10 Steps to the Perfect

SAT® Essay

2018-2019 Edition

ISBN-10: 1978226608; ISBN-13: 978-1978226609

Visit us at **PrepVantageBooks.com**

Table of Contents

CONTINUES ON THE NEXT PAGE

Additional Essay Content

About this book

We at PrepVantage set out to create this SAT Essay book with a few specific goals in mind. The first, naturally, was to offer a rigorous and comprehensive treatment of the SAT Essay itself, a test requirement that is absolutely necessary for a variety of top-tier colleges. But while a good essay is a sign of writing prowess, solid essay scores should not be reserved for the "select few." With sound strategies and thoughtful practice, students at all levels can dramatically increase their Essay scores. Solid 8s in Reading, Analysis, and Writing require hard work. The right hard work, though, can make an 8 in each category a reality.

Yet as we traded notes and looked over recent high-scoring essays, we realized something more. It is true that the base SAT Essay assignment—analyze an author's argument and rhetorical techniques—has not changed at all since the New SAT made its 2016 debut. Standards, though, *have* changed behind the scenes. The high-scoring samples that appeared in the first College Board Official SAT book are no longer reliable guides. New formats for introductions and conclusions, and new forms of excellence in reading comprehension and sentence structure, have emerged since then.

This book is designed both to stabilize the experience of taking the SAT Essay and to respond to an important reality: as a portion of the test partially based on the judgments of readers, the essay can and will change over time. We have drawn on the most up-to-date material on the market; as the years go by, our series will continue to update and expand. For now, read on, knowing that this book is your key to the perfect SAT Essay—brought to you by people behind the ultimate test prep resource.

— PrepVantage Publishing
New York, January 2018

Chapter 1: Planning
The SAT Essay

Main Requirements

Each SAT Essay will ask you to address the same few tasks. In fact, one benefit of the format of the SAT Essay is that it is extremely predictable. Invariably, you will need to

1. Read a 650- to 750-word nonfiction passage (on a topic in social science, humanities, natural science, politics, or some combination of these disciplines)
2. Identify the author's main argument (since the passage will ALWAYS have a strong thesis) and the methods used to build and convey that argument
3. Write an essay of your own (ALWAYS five paragraphs for a reasonably good score) explaining how the author constructed a solid argumentative position using logic, evidence, credibility, writing style, appeals to emotion, or other devices

The Grading Scheme for each essay will be as follows:

Total SAT Essay Score	Score by Each Reader (2 Assigned)	Subscores (3 Areas)
24-6	12-3	Reading (4-1) Analysis (4-1) Writing (4-1)

While the Total Essay Score may seem like the number that matters the most, securing this score in the top range requires excellent work in each of the subscore areas. Unfortunately, it is possible for an essay to have an excellent subscore (4) in one area and a middling (3) or sub-par (2) subscore in another. To see why, consider each subscore on its own.

Reading

This category tests how well you have comprehended the author's main idea and responded to the principal techniques of the passage. In short, do you get the big picture?

Analysis

This category tests how well you can delve into the author's reasoning and work with specific quotations. In short, can you explain the nuances of what the author is doing?

Writing

This category tests your own grammar, vocabulary, sentence structure, and overall essay structure and coherence. In short, are you reasonably eloquent as a writer?

Length, Timing, and Traps

First of all, remember that you have 50 MINUTES to read the passage and write the essay. That is plenty of time, but you should learn to pace yourself to make every minute count.

Second of all, keep in mind that the College Board Readers will spend VERY LITTLE TIME with your writing. Overall, 1.5-3 minutes is a good estimate for how long they will spend with each essay. Much of your writing will, naturally, need to leave a powerful first impression. Here are a few ways to make an impact.

Write 3-4 pages worth of content while maintaining good quality

Why should you?

Although many of the SAT Essay readers will have a rubric and its standards in mind, the instinct will be to reward the essays that are most fully structured and developed. You NEED to pace yourself for an essay that fleshes out your ideas. The easy assumption, for most readers, will be that a much longer essay does a better job of breaking down and fully engaging the prompt.

Of course, you could write a brilliant essay in only two pages. But readers who read quickly and who (if only subconsciously) are trained to reward longer essays may never catch on. Trust us: more is more.

> # Spend roughly 10 Minutes
> # reading and annotating the essay

Why should you?

Read and annotate wisely, and the essay will fall beautifully into place. With practice, you will learn to pinpoint the writer's main techniques and devices. If you underline them and comprehend them as you go, you will have an effectively marked-up essay that you can revisit for quotations and ideas.

If you don't annotate, you will be in for a lot of confusing re-reading and re-thinking. Save yourself the trouble: pinpoint what you want to talk about on the first run through.

> # Make sure you write EXACTLY
> # FIVE PARAGRAPHS

Why should you?

In theory, you could write a brilliant essay with a different number of paragraphs. In practice, it rarely happens. Readers will be expecting the standard five-paragraph, three-part-thesis structure. Just go with it and watch the high scores roll in.

What's more, virtually every SAT Essay book on the market recommends it. Four paragraphs appear hasty; six are distracting and are a nuisance to coordinate. Five: perfect.

And now, a few traps to ALWAYS avoid.

NEVER bring in <u>personal experience</u> or <u>outside knowledge</u>

Why is this so bad?

The SAT Essay tests your ability to understand and analyze a source. This is NOT a test of knowledge, or of your own ability to put together an argument. Anything beyond the passage text will be a distraction.

If you have been trained to use an outside quotation as a hook, or personal experience in your conclusions, you will NEED to break these habits. Your essay scores will thank you later.

NEVER give your <u>OPINION</u> (beyond indicating that the passage is effective)

Why is this so bad?

Opinions, like outside knowledge and personal experience, are major distractions. In fact, they can be much worse: they can undermine your entire essay. You may not agree with the arguments in some of the passages you read, but pointing out weaknesses has NOTHING to do with the essay assignment.

Only one type of opinion is allowed: affirming that the passage is effective. After all, SAT Essay passages are selected based on high standards of logical coherence. Pointing out that the passage was well-crafted is not really an "outside opinion": it is a statement in line with the test's own premises.

Reading and Note-Taking

In terms of how you approach the essay, there are a few tricks that can make your reading and note-taking process much easier.

MAIN IDEA

BEFORE reading the essay, figure out the author's main idea. The College Board has a funny habit of giving away this main idea in a directions box at the end of each passage, as shown below.

Write an essay in which you explain how Julian Strauss builds an argument to persuade his audience that arts funding practices are fundamentally flawed. In your essay, analyze how Strauss uses one or more of the features listed in the box above (or features of your own choice) to strengthen the logic and persuasiveness of his argument. Be sure that your analysis focuses on the most relevant features of the passage. *Main Idea*

Your essay should not explain whether you agree with Strauss's claims, but rather explain how Strauss builds an argument to persuade his audience.

Whatever occurs after the words "[his/her] audience that..." will be the basic main idea, and should help you with comprehension.

HOWEVER, keep in mind that simply reiterating this basic main idea will NOT guarantee you a strong Reading score. By now, plenty of essay writers—including some who are not all that good—know this trick. To lock down this scoring category, you need to demonstrate comprehension that goes beyond the wording in the box. You can read more about our reasoning starting on page 18, if you want to skip ahead.

Of course, use the box at the end to figure out the thesis quickly. Just don't depend on it for much more than that.

AUTHOR'S TECHNIQUES

As you move through the passage, UNDERLINE instances of the main techniques that the author uses to build his or her argument. The directions call attention to a few techniques that you might prioritize.

College Board Techniques (3 Given)

- Evidence
- Reasoning
- Stylistic or Persuasive Elements

HOWEVER, we at PrepVantage prioritize a somewhat different set of techniques. The College Board directions leave out some of the most potent writing devices (such as credibility). Also, if you write one Evidence paragraph and one Reasoning paragraph, you may wind up with two paragraphs that (quite by accident) are extremely similar. Both Reasoning and Evidence, after all, are premised on the same broader category, Logic.

Here are the Author's Techniques categories that we prefer.

RECOMMENDED Techniques (3 of Your Choice)

- Logic
- Credibility
- Style
- Emotion

Of course, you can modify or re-combine some of these categories once you are accustomed to the SAT Essay. But as you will see once you reach the chapters on our categories, you will STILL need to analyze different techniques with high precision, exactly as we do in this book.

High-Scoring Tactics

To excel on the SAT Essay, you must begin with the right mindset. In essence, you must be able to defend yourself against common errors BEFORE you even write your first essay.

Yes, that sounds like some sort of Jedi mind trick. But we at PrepVantage have seen enough SAT Essays to know that there are certain features that can reliably distinguish a 3 (middle-of-the-road) from a 4 (highest-scoring) on any given subsection. If you know what these are in advance, you will be better able to train yourself in the mindset that you need to get solid 4s from any reader the College Board sends your way.

Explaining the Passage

Top Score (4)	Middling Score (3)
Uses the main idea from the box as the basis for more insightful comprehension	Relies almost entirely on the main idea from the directions box for comprehension
Addresses the overall structure and passage techniques as part of the synopsis	Vague or sketchy about structure or techniques, at least until the body paragraphs

Working with Quotations

Top Score (4)	Middling Score (3)
Important quotations chosen selectively to build up body paragraphs	Chosen quotations seem haphazardly selected (and may even be over-used)
Analysis responds sensitively to the significance of each quotation	Analysis, though used for each quotation, is quick and sketchy (or relies on generalities)
Quotations introduced in a correct and fluid manner; citations (if used at all) do not distract	Quotations introduced clearly, but at times awkwardly or with needless citations

Grammar and Wording

Top Score (4)	Middling Score (3)
No obvious and elementary misspellings	Some misspellings, but not distracting overall
Effective uses of parallelism, subordinate clauses, semicolons, and other devices for coordinating longer sentences	Effective uses of basic sentence devices (subject-verb agreement, pronoun agreement), but few successful or attempted longer sentences

Style and Vocabulary

Top Score (4)	Middling Score (3)
Uses advanced vocabulary that is entirely appropriate to the essay task	Uses simpler vocabulary fairly effectively (or may misuse more advanced words)
Sentence openings, structures, and lengths are impressively varied	Sentences are easy to understand, but are simpler or monotonous
Repeats phrasing directly from the instruction boxes once AT THE ABSOLUTE MOST	Repeats phrasing directly from the instruction boxes frequently and awkwardly

You can see these standards in action in the high-scoring student responses gathered in Appendix B and Appendix C. More importantly, keep these standards in mind as you begin writing your own essays. That process begins, from the Main Idea down, in the next chapter.

Chapter 2:
The Main Idea

Grasping the Main Idea

As we noted in the previous chapter, each SAT Essay will be accompanied by a directions box (right at the end of the passage) that provides the basic main idea.

Remember the trick from earlier? Just look right after the words "persuade [his/her] audience that . . ." for a very good synopsis of the author's argument

Write an essay in which you explain how Margaret Hensley builds an argument to persuade her audience that adjunct teaching is a fulfilling career choice. In your essay, analyze how Hensley uses one or more of the features listed in the box above (or features of your own choice) to strengthen the logic and persuasiveness of her argument. Be sure that your analysis focuses on the most relevant features of the passage.

Your essay should not explain whether you agree with Hensley's claims, but rather explain how Hensley builds an argument to persuade her audience.

Main Idea

Go to this main idea BEFORE you read the passage. This synopsis can help you comprehend even the toughest essays

This basic main idea is helpful, but you need to keep in mind one reality of SAT Essay scoring.

Repeating the main idea in the box DOES NOT guarantee a high score

Nor should it. Finding that main idea is an extremely common trick; even the worst SAT tutor on the planet probably knows the "go to the box" ploy. So use the box, but do NOT grow completely reliant on it as you write.

To demonstrate a nuanced sense of main idea—and thus earn a high Reading score—you will need to delve deeper into the passage you have been given. There are a few strategies for doing so. And the first, in fact, begins with that notorious box.

Tactic 1

It the very least, RE-STATE the box main idea in your OWN words

The first way to express comprehension of the Main Idea is a bit simpler than the others. It also works especially well if you have good vocabulary. Instead of thinking about the Main Idea from the ground up, find new words to express what the author has stated.

There are a few obvious benefits to this method.

- Extremely straightforward
- Also helps your Writing score
- Great if you are pressed for time

Indeed, aggressively re-wording the Main Idea may be the best INITIAL strategy for some test-takers, considering its simplicity and directness. The other tactics, though potent, are somewhat more subtle. Keep in mind, though, that the re-wording needs to be both ACCURATE and ELEGANT. Those qualities can take practice.

Take a look at the main idea of an essay that will be referenced throughout this book, "The Self-Driving Collision Course" by Tim Sorelson

> Write an essay in which you explain how Tim Sorelson builds an argument to persuade his audience that the widespread adoption of self-driving cars would be counterproductive. In your essay, analyze how Sorelson uses one or more of the features listed in the box above (or features of your own choice) to strengthen the logic and persuasiveness of his argument. Be sure that your analysis focuses on the most relevant features of the passage.
>
> Your essay should not explain whether you agree with Sorelson's claims, but rather explain how Sorelson builds an argument to persuade his audience.

the widespread adoption of self-driving cars would be counterproductive

You do NOT want your reader to see the phrase "the widespread adoption of self-driving cars would be counterproductive" to the point of nausea. So, take those concepts, and find interesting ways to re-express them.

- the proliferation of self-driving cars would be problematic
- autonomous car technology would be detrimental to its users
- self-driving vehicles should not be used throughout society

These ideas are virtually identical in meaning to the Main Idea. Yet they employ new vocabulary and approximate OTHER ideas from the passage ("technology, "society") as a pleasant side effect. If you have read the passage effectively, such elementary re-wording CAN become a first step in demonstrating very deep comprehension.

Tactic 2

> # Begin with the Main Idea in the Box, and start asking "WHY?"

Instead of reiterating the main idea and leaving it at that, start delving into the author's ideas. The natural way to do this is simply to start asking why an author takes a specific position. What motivates the author? What justifies or drives the argument as a whole?

These questions, if addressed well, indicate deep comprehension. To see the power of asking "why?" as an essay-writing method, consider once again the main idea from Sorelson's essay.

the widespread adoption of self-driving cars would be counterproductive

Okay. But WHY does Sorelson oppose the "widespread adoption of self-driving cars?" Take a look at the essay itself in Appendix B (starting on page 118) and try to figure out the main justifications.

Some of Sorelson's principal, over-arching reasons for his position are the following.

21

1. Faulty assumptions behind the "benefits" of self-driving cars

2. Lack of corporate leadership to promote self-driving cars

3. Record of failed experiments with self-driving technology

None of this is directly evident from the simple Main Idea in the box. But ALL of this can be determined by asking "why?" in a strategic manner—and indicates outstanding comprehension of the essay at hand.

Tactic 3

Pinpoint the topic and ask yourself "WHAT IS THE SIGNIFICANCE?"

Here, your task is to figure out what the importance of the essay is (without, of course, pulling in distracting outside knowledge). You must figure out something beyond what the author's ideas are: what, exactly, is important about these ideas?

For this version of advanced understanding, return to the Sorelson essay. Again, start with the main idea.

the widespread adoption of self-driving cars would be counterproductive

Now, WHAT IS THE IMPORTANCE of any of this? Well, if you put Sorelson's essay in perspective, the drawbacks of self-driving cars are significant for a few reasons.

1. Self-driving cars involve flawed, controversial technology

2. Consumers could be harmed by the current self-driving formats

3. Proponents of self-driving cars wrongly overlook significant drawbacks

Discussing broad significance is an excellent way to show that you have thought through the nuances, implications, and repercussions of an issue. But explaining significance also allows you to address those who might QUESTION the importance of a passage. As it turns out, addressing other, opposing perspectives is yet another way to prove advanced comprehension.

Tactic 4

What are OBJECTIONS to this idea and why are the objections WRONG?

If you have been trained to understand and analyze counter-arguments in one of your English courses, this can be a reliable method. A truly complex main idea isn't a blunt, one-note statement. Rather, the Main Ideas that you will see on the SAT Essay passages respond to large debates—and the authors are usually AWARE of their opposition.

Explaining some of these features can reflect very well on your comprehension and thoughtfulness as a reader. To see how, take another look at the writing from Sorelson and keep his main idea in mind. In fact, working with basic tones can be a highly effective approach here.

What might be some principal OBJECTIONS to the main argument about the problems with self-driving cars? Here are a few, based either on the passage or on basic logic (or on both).

1. Self-driving cars are useful technology
2. Self-driving cars will promote innovation

These are major points that might be brought against Sorelson's idea. But remember, your task is NEVER to argue against the author. Instead, you need to explain how Sorelson's argument,ADDRESSES and OVERCOMES these objections. Doing so is not very difficult, once you have read the passage.

1. EXAMINE the passage for its overarching strengths
2. OPPOSE the objections with specific features of the passage

You are, in essence, shooting down any arguments against the author that you can think of, all with the purpose of showing the strength of the author's main idea. Here is how to deal with the objections to Sorelson.

1. Self-driving cars are useful technology; NO, they have not evolved to the point of being ready for general use
2. Self-driving cars will promote innovation; NO, they have promoted misconceptions and are linked to controversy

Also, keep in mind that authors may THEMSELVES address the other side. Sorelson does so in paragraphs 1-3 (roughly) of his essay. Raising and disproving objections can become very easy, if the author does some of the work. For essays that discuss counter-arguments as prominently as Sorelson's does, the process of raising and refuting will also, as a happy side-effect, read as a savvy response to one of the author's own major strategies.

Presenting the Main Idea

As important as the Main Idea is, there are only two real portions of the essay that call for you to articulate it.

1. The Introduction
2. The Conclusion

You will need to deliver concise, original statements about the thesis of the passage that you have just read at each of these two points. Fortunately, you can use the tactics in this chapter to address these portions of your writing easily. Try something like this for variety.

Main Idea Strategy

1. Use one of Tactics 1-4 when writing your introduction
2. Try to use a DIFFERENT Tactic (again 1-4) when writing your conclusion

You will see exactly this kind of well-developed approach to Main Ideas in high-scoring essays. If you want, consider the TEMPLATES later in the book (page 31 for the Introduction, page 74 for the Conclusion). But a good introduction does MORE than demonstrate comprehension as you see in the next chapter—which is all about introductions, naturally.

Chapter 3:
The Introduction

Main Requirements

In order to write an effective introduction, keep a few fundamental standards in mind.

1. High-scoring introductions average THREE sentences, possibly four if you are dealing with a relatively complex passage or thesis.
2. An excellent introduction will always list the AUTHOR (first and last name), TITLE, and MAIN IDEA of the essay.
3. Every proficient introduction will end with a thesis statement in the LAST sentence, which sets up the three body paragraphs.

The endpoint of an effective introduction should be clear to any student who has written a five-paragraph, three-part-thesis essay. But getting there can be a more difficult matter. However, just keep in mind a few pieces of advice, and all difficulties will vanish.

STARTING POINT:
Main Idea, Author, Title

For the first two sentences of the introduction, you have some liberty in terms of organization, if you want. But there are three elements that are indispensable:

In TWO Sentences

1. **Author's Full Name**

2. **Article's Main Title**

3. **Explanation of the Main Idea**

These tasks should be divided between the two sentences quite efficiently. While you can use a format of your own to address these requirements, the format below accomplishes everything noted above in a straightforward manner.

Sentence 1

• Author's Full Name (1), Main Title (2), BASIC Statement of Main Idea (3)

Sentence 2

• FURTHER Statement of Main Idea (only 3)

In essence, you should use Sentence 1 to present basic information and the fundamentals of comprehension. Don't delve into the complexities of the main idea here, either. Instead, you could use a highly accurate RE-WORDING of the main idea in the box at the end (Main Idea Tactic 1, page 19).

For the second sentence, use Main Idea Tactic 2, 3, or 4 to establish DEEPER comprehension. But make sure to keep this stage efficient. You need to move at a steady clip towards the all-important third sentence that finishes the introduction, your thesis.

FINISH POINT:
Your Essay's Thesis

The thesis for your essay will function just like the thesis of a classic five-paragraph essay. It will provide a decisive statement, return to the main topic, and set up all three of your body paragraphs. Try to think of it as a one-sentence guide to where your entire essay must go.

So what is your thesis, structure-wise?

BASIC IDEA

The AUTHOR effectively supports his or her MAIN IDEA through the use of DEVICE 1, DEVICE 2, and DEVICE 3.

To fulfill these standards, keep the following rules in mind.

> **Your thesis statement MUST explain ALL THREE body paragraph topics**

If the thesis doesn't, you will be left with an essay that seems very disorganized—at least to readers who read as quickly as those at the College Board.

But make sure to keep in mind one other rule, for the sake of clarity.

A thesis that fulfills all of these requirements will effectively lead into the essay. And to make sure that your thesis avoids any confusion or awkwardness, keep the following content and style guidelines in mind.

Make sure that your devices are DISTINCT

The last thing that you want is a thesis that seems to line up three devices that are interchangeable. Such a statement will only confuse the reader. As you mark up the passage, be sure that you have different but well-developed ideas.

Don't use devices that are almost interchangeable.

- facts about science, facts about research, and statistics. X

or that are confusingly similar in type.

- style, persuasive elements, and word choice. X

If, in contrast, you can create a thesis and thus an essay that call attention to a range of different tactics, you will demonstrate strong comprehension. You will also avoid a troubling sense of redundancy in the crucial early stages of the essay.

- counter-arguments, appeals to pity, and demonstrations of scientific expertise. ✔

Explain your ideas using PARALLEL STRUCTURE

Always, to demonstrate strong command of sentence structure, put your ideas in the thesis in parallel.

- using statistics, counter-arguments, and because he uses appeals to authority. X

- statistics, through the use of counter-arguments, and appeals to authority. X

Parallelism is after all one of the important topics on the SAT Writing and Language test. If you fail to exhibit effect parallelism on the Essay, readers will question your command of SAT fundamentals.

Quite simply, for this important sentence, make sure that your three devices are explained using three versions of the same structure. Three nouns or three prepositional phrases, as in the examples below, can be very good approaches.

- using statistics, counter-arguments, and appeals to authority **(parallel nouns)** ✔

- by presenting valid statistics, by examining counter-arguments, and by appealing to his own authority as a researcher **(parallel short phrases)** ✔

NOW, PUT EVERYTHING TOGETHER

Just consult the template on the next page for a fill-in-the-blanks guide to the SAT Essay introduction.

Or, to see the introduction in practice, turn to the sample essay introduction on page 32.

Template

Sentence 1:

As [AUTHOR] demonstrates in "[TITLE]," [FIRST STATEMENT FROM MAIN IDEA].

Sentence 2:

However, the significance of [AUTHOR]'s chosen issue does not end there; for him/her, [SECOND STATEMENT FROM MAIN IDEA].

Sentence 3:

[AUTHOR] effectively establishes and substantiates his/her argument about [MAIN IDEA] by employing [DEVICE 1], by using [DEVICE 2], and by presenting [DEVICE 3].

Sample Introduction

From the SAT Essay Response in Appendix B (Page 123)

As Tim Sorelson demonstrates in "The Self-Driving Collision Course," adopting self-driving cars as a new norm in modern transportation would create major problems for consumers and companies. However, the significance of Sorelson's chosen issue does not end there; for him, the reality that self-driving cars are counterproductive contradicts common fantasies about these vehicles. Sorelson effectively establishes and substantiates his argument against self-driving car usage by employing case studies about major companies, by using direct address, and by presenting the faulty counter-arguments of his opponents.

An introduction that follows this template will fit the most recent length standards, will contain a unified thesis, and will exhibit some effective turns of comprehension and sentence structure.

However, it will NOT have one introduction feature that you may be accustomed to: a hook. But do you really need one?

Can you use a hook?

This is a very good question. If you have been taught to write using a hook, you can try one as your first sentence. But keep in mind that.

> ## A hook is NOT in fact necessary and MAY WEAKEN your essay

Now, why is this the case?

1. Few Recent High-Scoring Essays Use Hooks

Of the outstanding essays posted by the College Board, the Khan Academy, and the SAT Essay books that appeared before this one, VERY FEW use hooks. The prevailing SAT Essay standard is to demonstrate good, quick comprehension and hit the body paragraphs. That's it.

Naturally, these standards MAY change over time. Some of the better essays in the 2016 Edition of the Official SAT book did, in fact, use rudimentary hooks. If the standards change, we will be prepared. But for 2018, hooks are mostly out.

2. Very Few Types of Effective Hooks Are Possible

Many of the standard hooks rely information that is OFF-LIMITS for the SAT Essay: personal anecdotes, bits of unusual trivial, metaphors, spins on well-known sayings, famous quotations, definitions. All of these are forms of outside knowledge, and are thus major distractions.

Only two SAT Essay hooks, really, are viable.

1. A QUESTION that leads into the passage

2. A QUOTATION addressing a major issue from the passage

As you can see, these two are very much oriented towards the passage itself. They may lend some variety in tone and structure (since you won't, naturally, be using questions elsewhere in your response). But there is a third liability that can undermine even a good hook of this sort.

3. The Hook Must Be Effectively Linked to the Paragraph

Coordinating a hook can be a very AWKWARD process, from a stylistic standpoint. You don't want to expend sentences explaining your hook, but you don't want to leave it dangling without any context either. Striking the right balance is very difficult and can take you well beyond three or even four sentences.

In short, be EXTREMELY cautious of hooks. Still, if they do start making a comeback, we'll be the first to let you know.

Chapter 4: Devices
Logic and Credibility

The Strategy

Most of the passages that you will encounter on the SAT Essay will be premised on two traits that you should use to your advantage.

1. They will be organized using highly logical chains of reasoning and orderly overall structures
2. They will be written by authors who are clearly credible or authoritative

Keep in mind that, for timing and efficiency

> **you MUST UNDERLINE logic and credibility AS YOU READ, not after**

Your task will be to make the most of these built-in assets. As you read through each essay prompt, it will be up to you to extract strong instances of logic and credibility; then, explain HOW these samples function and WHY they are significant in building up the passage's main idea.

Working with Logic and Credibility

As you work through each SAT Essay, you should locate the devices that support the author's argument in a logical fashion. These include

- Examples that offer concrete proof supporting the main idea
- Cause-and-effect reasoning that demonstrates repercussions
- Statistics and measures that provide empirical evidence
- Responses to counter-arguments and possible objections
- Acknowledgments of trade-offs and advantages/liabilities

You should also be prepared to discuss how the author establishes himself or herself as a credible source. Some devices include

- Referencing personal accomplishments, positions, or credentials
- Discussing projects by the author that relate directly to the topic of the essay
- Elaborating personal experiences that demonstrate the author's firsthand knowledge of the issues
- Setting forward a moral commitment to the topic at hand
- Establishing the author as a source of thoughtful and pragmatic advice

---

YOUR ESSAY TASK

IDENTIFY linked or complementary instances of logic or credibility as you read the essay passage

EXPLAIN and CONNECT these instances in well-coordinated paragraphs

---

On the pages that follow, we have pinpointed some of the forms of logic and credibility that appear most prominently in SAT Essay passages. We have also explained the significance of these forms. While significance can vary from essay to essay, authors do tend to use some of these devices in similar ways. You can take this information as a guide, but always make sure to adapt it to individual essays.

Remember also to vary your vocabulary when discussing logic and credibility. If you need stylistic tips for these elements of the SAT Essay, please consult the materials on pages 92-110.

Note-Taking Tip

as you underline, CLASSIFY each instance and briefly NOTE its significance

If you follow this tip, you will essentially perform some of your analysis IN ADVANCE. Writing the essay (especially the challenging sections about significance) becomes easy when you have clear, precise notes to consult.

So what is the most efficient way to start understanding why these devices matter? Significance may of course vary from essay prompt to essay prompt. Overall, though, each device will be important for a few standard reasons—which are outlined in the charts that follow.

Charts begin on the next page

Statistics	Significance
	Impart specific measures and figures to issues that might otherwise remain vague or abstract (logic)
	Clarify the scope, impact, or severity of specific issues or problems for the reader (logic)
	Demonstrate that the author is in command of precise and empirically valid information (credibility)

Linked Examples	Significance
	Indicate that the author's ideas are relevant across a range of activities or disciplines (logic)
	Vouch for the magnitude of the author's chosen topic as one that plays out similarly even in a diversity of contexts (logic)
	Suggest the breadth of the author's knowledge and perspective (credibility)

Repercussions and Consequences	Significance
	Show that the author is drawing rational linkages that explain and map out the issue at hand (logic)
	Help the reader to see that the events or occurrences considered by the author have specific, well-articulated, and meaningful cause-and-effect relationships (logic)

Addressing the Opposing Argument	Significance
	Enables the writer to directly confront and eliminate faulty, deceptive, or absurd lines of argumentation (logic)
	Indicates the strength of the writer's own reasoning, since clear counter-arguments can be addressed without undermining the thesis (logic/credibility)
	Introduces a sense of balance, rationality, and broad perspective, since the writer can see and understand the opposite viewpoint (logic/credibility)

Research and Experiments	Significance
	Give the reader a walk-through of well-organized procedures and principles, with the eventual goal of showing a measurable and well-explained outcome (logic)
	Lend validity and rigor to discussions that a reader may otherwise see as subjective, ESPECIALLY for humanities, culture, and politics (credibility)

Solution to a Problem	Significance
	Demonstrates that the author has created a rigorous chain of reasoning that culminates in a well-defined proposal (logic)
	Indicates that the author possesses specialized knowledge that can be used constructively (credibility)
	Introduces a tone of pragmatism that counteracts the possibility of an overly critical or pessimistic argument (credibility)

Professional, Official, or Academic Position	Significance
	Establishes that the author is an expert recognized by other experts, who may (at least implicitly) agree with his or her claims and methods (credibility)
	Provides meaningful background and context for the author's accomplishments or knowledge regarding a specific field (credibility)

Approval of Other Experts	Significance
	Functions much like linked examples in showing that the writer's conclusions are supported by a mass of rigorous research and inquiry (logic/credibility)
	Demonstrates that the writer is a conscientious or well-received authority among authorities (credibility)
	Shows the writer's appreciation of the subtleties of inquiry, research, and professionalism regarding the chosen issue (credibility)

Firsthand Testimony	Significance
	Clarifies the main idea for the reader by showing how the author drew conclusions from specific observations and impressions (logic)
	Suggests that the author's involvement in the issue at hand is direct and highly active, NOT motivated by a distant or passive approach that would call the author's commitment and authority into question (credibility)

Ethical or Moral Values	Significance
	Present the author as a model of conduct and righteousness for the reader to admire and perhaps follow (credibility)
	Affirm the author's commitment to and immersion in the topic, since the writing is motivated by a strong sense of moral and ethical responsibility (credibility)

Chapter 5: Devices
Style and Emotion

The Strategy

In the previous chapter, you were given an intensive look at the fundamental tactics that authors use to write sensible, coherent, rational essays. However, in order to write essays that are appealing in other ways—that are eloquent, moving, and memorable on a word-by-word level—authors will resort to a set of very different devices. For the purposes of the SAT Essay, those devices can be placed in two major categories.

1. Subtle stylistic features involving word choice, sentence structure, repetition, punctuation, and other means of creating verbal interest and emphasis

2. Striking emotional features that are meant to convey the writer's own cogent feelings, or to evoke specific feelings in the reader

Working with Style and Emotion

Some of the SAT Essays that you encounter will be motived by extremely strong, extremely obvious emotions. Hope, sadness, anger, affection, disgust, and joy are but a few of the powerful feelings that will arise. If you do face an extremely emotional essay, consider the following tactics.

- Read for the MAIN emotions and define them precisely
- Consider how these emotions engage the reader

However, you may be presented with an essay that seems much more cut-and-dry. If this is the case, you might consider the nuanced stylistic features that will enhance even a relatively detached piece of writing

- Repetition of sounds, punctuation, words, or phrases
- Imagery, scenes, or anecdotes that serve narrative purposes
- Engaging ways of addressing the audience ("you," "we")

In fact, you can consider stylistic features such as word choice and sentence structure in ANY essay. Use these aspects of close reading to pinpoint the most subtle points of the author's message.

YOUR ESSAY TASK

IDENTIFY the emotions that the author expresses, and the recurring or prominent stylistic devices

DEMONSTRATE the significance of these features in unified (1 minimum, 2 maximum) body paragraphs

---

Emotion Techniques

The first essential of working with the emotions that an SAT Essay author uses involves both a piece of advice and a warning.

> ## Identify precise emotions, but DO NOT over-think those emotions

It is NEVER enough to say something vague and useless along the lines of "the author uses emotional appeals" or "the author is highly emotional" and leave your discussion at that. You MUST figure out whether the author is using hope, anger, pity, or some other specific, well-defined emotion. And you must ALSO pinpoint that emotion in a topic sentence if you decide to give that emotion a paragraph.

Yet make sure to avoid the opposite danger. You have probably seen from your English courses that even a single statement can have a variety of emotional meanings, depending on how it is interpreted. Finding such a variety of meanings is NOT required on the SAT. In fact, if you admit that a statement is emotionally ambiguous or ambivalent, you will often WEAKEN your ability to analyze the SAT Essay passage with clarity.

Simply follow these steps.

1. As you read through the passage, NOTE the author's main EMOTIONS

2. CLASSIFY those emotions as POSITIVE or NEGATIVE

3. DETERMINE the SIGNIFICANCE of those emotions

To achieve all of this, you can consult the charts in this chapter: some are for positive emotions, others for negative.

NOTE:

Some essay passages may be predominantly negative or positive in the emotions that they use. Such essays can create extremely clear and coherent emotion paragraphs.

However, an essay that SHIFTS emotions may do so for important reasons, such as to guide the reader's own loyalties or to lead into a solution to a problem. Analyzing a shift can be a very useful tactic, if you identify exactly HOW the emotions shift from one to another.

Now, you are ready to explore how these emotions are significant. Just turn to the charts that begin on page 51.

Positive Emotions

Joy/ Pleasure	Significance
	Communicates to the reader the author's enthusiasm for and deep commitment to the topic at hand
	Generates excitement and emphasis when linked to scenic, sensory, and episodic descriptions
	Lends emotional vitality and spontaneity to a topic that (in some essays) may be difficult or technical

Hope/ Optimism	Significance
	Construes the author as humanistic and forward thinking, and thus wins the reader's admiration
	Counteracts the possibility (a clear danger of some essays) of an overwhelmingly negative tone

Positive Emotions

Pride/ Patriotism/ Fellowship	Significance
	Defines in a positive and welcoming manner a group identity that the author (and reader) should find appealing
	Grounds the author's analysis in a positive, inspiring values system that has already gained followers and firm support
	Effectively balances out critical content with proactive, "call to arms" appeals

Accessibility/ Friendliness/ Good Humor	Significance
	Helps the writer to seem welcoming and approachable (not just passionate or logical)
	Entertains the reader with light-hearted or clever moments
	Results in vivid everyday references (normal events, pop culture, etc.) that help the reader to grasp the passage's argument

Negative Emotions

Anger/ Outrage	Significance
	Shows that the author is confident enough in the righteousness of his or her ideas to invite conflict or controversy
	Alerts the reader to the urgency and gravity of the issues that the author has chosen to address
	Indicates that the author's opponents deserve harsh, serious disapproval on moral grounds

Anxiety/ Urgency/ Fear	Significance
	Underscore potentially destructive implications and consequences related to the author's chosen topic
	Indicate that the reader, following the author's lead, should harbor deep concerns about the issues raised in the passage

Negative Emotions

Sadness/ Pity	Significance
	Addresses consequential though perhaps "technical" or "abstract" problems on a deeply humane and involved level
	Helps to single out individuals who deserve both the author's and the reader's compassion
	Construes the writer as righteous, engaged, and unafraid of candid expressions of feeling

Contempt/ Cynicism/ Sarcasm	Significance
	Highlights the absurd or destructive qualities of ideas that the writer opposes
	Adds complexity to the writer's tone through negative irony and humor, but adds passion and emphasis to the writer's stance as well

Style Techniques

Working with stylistic features—the fine points of HOW the essay passage is written—can be useful in a few ways. In fact, there are two somewhat divergent ends that stylistic analysis can serve.

1. Stylistic analysis can COMPLEMENT analysis of EMOTION

2. Stylistic analysis can be effective ON ITS OWN

When to use each type of analysis is, to some extent, a matter of the essay type that you are considering.

Tactic 1

If you are addressing an essay passage with STRONG emotions (an impassioned political speech, for instance), try this one. You can discuss how the author uses specific devices to communicate powerful feelings. Here, the emotions are so prominent that analysis of style can be used to complement the broader analysis of an author's emotions.

Tactic 2

If you are addressing an essay passage with WEAK emotions or an apparently DETACHED tone (an argument in favor of a complex public health policy, for instance), try this one. Emotions such as joy, anger, and sarcasm may not stand out. However, a more reserved author will still use subtle turns of writing to impress and intrigue a reader. Stylistic analysis can call attention to such features, AND can sometimes reveal the subtle emotions beneath a seemingly unemotional passage.

Questions	Significance
	Urge the reader to think actively and deeply about an issue, rather than allowing a passive or non-engaged response
	Put special emphasis on important ideas and turning points, since questions will be relatively rare and will thus stand out
	In the case of rhetorical questions, show how the author has firmly and passionately embraced a strong stance, and has passionately rejected the alternatives

Colloquial or Informal Expressions	Significance
	Help the author to seem accessible or approachable in a manner that wins the reader's loyalty or goodwill
	Counterbalance any technical or challenging material by showing that the author has an easygoing, innate, or human connection to the topic

Repeating Sentence Structure	Significance
	Highlights central ideas and makes them memorable by placing them in rhythmic, emphatic phrases
	Gives a sense of regularity and control to the author's argument, and indicates that the author can eloquently connect concepts
	Communicates the author's passion by giving an urgent, at times "oratorical" quality to the author's most dramatic points

Scenic Imagery and Descriptions	Significance
	Present the reader with sights and spectacles that are rich in straightforward emotional meaning or intensity
	Provide a concrete and especially vivid way of envisioning author's chosen issue
	Appeal to sensory data and raw responses, and win over readers through descriptive prowess

Personal Anecdotes	Significance
	Create a more vivid and memorable presentation of evidence than analysis or explanation alone
	Invite the reader to understand the author's primary points from candid and uniquely approachable perspective

Collective Voice ("We")	**Significance**
	Indicates that the writer feels a connection to the reader (or some other group) and has a strong stake in the issues at hand
	Can be used to passionately call the reader or some other group to real, empowered action
	Generates an appealing sense of unity, cooperation, and community among the author and the author's supporters

Direct Address ("You")	**Significance**
	Can create the sense that the author is engaging the reader on a personal, directly emotional level
	May also help the author address the reader's presumed ideas and beliefs, either to express solidarity or to passionately offer correction
	Adds a colloquial and personable touch to the discussion as a whole

Metaphors and Similes	Significance
	Serve as vivid and accessible methods of illustrating ideas, including potentially difficult or distant concepts
	Showcase the author's talent for thinking in imaginative terms, often in a manner that pleases and impresses the reader
	Create (if the chosen imagery recurs or repeats) an original perspective on the issue while imparting unity to the passage

Short and Emphatic Sentences	Significance
	Create points of verbal stress in the passage, often to highlight especially important ideas
	Counterbalance longer sentences in a manner that makes the author's writing emphatic and direct

Caricature and Intended Exaggeration	Significance
	Create moments of humor that make the author seem clever, approachable, and appealing
	Can balance out more dire and serious content, adding diversity of tone to the writing
	Construe the author's opponents as laughable or ridiculous

Juxtaposition and Contrast	Significance
	Add clarity and impact to the author's most important concepts
	Help the writer to pair off positive and negative emotions in a way that indicates the dramatic, high-stakes nature of the issues at hand
	Elicit strong reactions in readers, who will be engaged by writing premised on clear conflicts or on stark differences

Chapter 6:
Body Paragraphs

Main Requirements

Regardless of the type of technique you are discussing—style, emotion, logic, or credibility—the three body paragraphs for your essay will be EXTREMELY formulaic. Each one will follow the same structure, essentially, as the others. And here is that structure, in a nutshell.

Sentence 1: TOPIC SENTENCE introducing the technique and affirming its significance

Sentence 2: Introduction of FIRST QUOTATION

Sentences 3-4: Significance of FIRST QUOTATION

Sentence 5: Introduction of SECOND QUOTATION

Sentences 6-7: Significance of SECOND QUOTATION

Sentence 8 (Optional): Overall Statement of Significance

Quick Note: Why is Sentence 8 Optional?

Some writers are very good at creating thoughtful "big picture" statements. If you are such a writer, providing an interesting and thought-provoking synopsis of the paragraph in Sentence 8 might be a good idea.

HOWEVER, some writers have a tendency to write summary statements that are merely repetitive and trite, even if those statements are accurate. If you feel that this is a danger, it might be better to keep the analysis flowing and to avoid Sentence 8 as a distraction.

Structuring Your Sentences

By the time you reach the body paragraphs, you should have the SAT Essay passage marked up with all of the essential information: AT LEAST quotes, IDEALLY some brief notes about their significance. The body paragraphs should feel as though they are falling into place.

The real challenges should be different matters:

1. Drawing connections and explaining significance insightfully
2. Writing sentences with advanced and varied vocabulary and structure

Challenge 1 is a matter of consistent practice. Now that you know some effective ways to group quotations and explain why they matter, you need to spend time getting comfortable with the methods by putting those methods into action.

Challenge 2 is also a matter of familiarity, but here it is helpful to see how the standards above play out even BEFORE you start practicing essay-by-essay.

w you can write varied, well-constructed sentences.
following structures.

~nce 1:

[AUTHOR] crafts a [adj. describing DEVICE] argument by incorporating [DEVICE] that illuminates his/her main topic: [TOPIC FROM MAIN IDEA].

Sentence 2:

In the course of his/her discussion, he/she asserts that "[QUOTATION 1]."

Sentences 3-4:

This information is intended to show the reader [SIGNIFICANCE, Q1], and to do so in a manner that [SIGNIFICANCE, Q1]. On account of [AUTHOR]'s evidence, readers can understand that [SIGNIFICANCE, Q1].

Sentence 5:

Yet [AUTHOR]'s use of [DEVICE 1] does not stop here; he/she continues on to explain that "[QUOTATION 2]."

Sentences 6-7:

With such a quotation, [AUTHOR] expands his/ her thesis outward to assert that [SIGNIFICANCE, Q2D1]. The true significance of such information is that it shows [SIGNIFICANCE, Q2D1].

Sentence 8 (Optional):

Together, these instances of [DEVICE] affirm that [AUTHOR] is a [CHOOSE: logical/authoritative/ cloquent/emotionally engaged] essayist, one adept in appealing to the reader's innate sense of [CHOOSE: rationality/expertise/moral authority/passion, fluid self-expression].

This paragraph template is taken from the first paragraph of the full SAT Essay template in Appendix A. The two other paragraphs that you will write follow exactly the same GENERAL IDEA, but need DIFFERENT SPECIFICS in terms of sentence structure and word choice to be fully effective as writing.

Now, consider how a full body paragraph (namely, the first of the three) will read if it is written according to this template.

Sample Body Paragraph

From the SAT Essay Response in Appendix B
(Pages 123-125)

Sorelson crafts a rigorous argument by incorporating

business-world evidence that illuminates his main

topic: self-driving cars are inadvisable. In the

course of his discussion, he asserts that one self-

driving "Tesla model . . . was at the center of a 2016

controversy, in which a Tesla on 'autopilot' crashed

into another car." This information is intended

to show the reader that self-driving technology

is fundamentally dangerous, and to do so in a

manner that portrays Sorelson as a knowledgeable

commentator. On account of Sorelson's evidence,

readers can understand that even prestigious

corporations cannot master self-driving technology.

Yet Sorelson's use of linked examples does not stop

here; he continues on to explain that other leading

self-driving companies are Google and Uber, "which

has been mired in corporate scandal for years."
With such a quotation, Sorelson expands his thesis
outward to assert that Tesla is not alone in mis-
managing self-driving cars. The true significance of
such information is that it shows how difficult it will
be to responsibly create self-driving vehicles, even
when companies with vast resources are involved.

Make sure that you use the OTHER TWO paragraphs in the template, too. In this way, each body paragraph will naturally fit the important stylistic rule from earlier.

EACH Body Paragraph needs different Sentence structures and lengths

Note that this paragraph OMITS Sentence 8. The reason for this is that a final, synoptic sentence may not be fully necessary if you master one final body paragraph tactic: transitions.

Transitions

Before we get to transitions that can effectively link paragraphs, let's consider the kinds of transitions that you should avoid entirely.

NEVER Use Simplistic Transitions

Even if the rest of your essay is working well, your writing will look childish if you use the following.

"First, . . . Second, . . . Third," for Body Paragraphs

"In conclusion," for the Conclusion

There is a lot wrong with these. The College Board readers are reasonably well-educated; NONE of them need to be told, in classic Captain Obvious fashion, that the last paragraph is the conclusion. Yes, writing "In conclusion," is not the worst SAT crime, but won't win over a reader who is having a bad day, or is between a 3 and a 4 in your Writing score. Don't take a chance.

Perhaps worse, these simplistic transitions may be read (or even misinterpreted) as signs that your writing technique has not evolved. You want good transitions, but if you are having transition troubles, you should not fall into a second transition trap.

NEVER Avoid Transitions Completely

You may be able to write your own academic essays effectively without obvious transitions. In fact, some of the best writers can establish an effortless, instinctive paragraph-to-paragraph flow. But this tactic will NOT work on the SAT.

Why? Simply put, College Board readers expect transitions, and take them as signs that you are actively and intelligently connecting ideas. An essay without clear transitions will just strike them as a choppy, disconnected read. It may not be so, but that is the quick-read impression that you will leave.

Fortunately, there are two broad types of mostly-effective SAT Essay transitions that you can bring into play.

USE Advanced Vocabulary Transitions

The transitions that quality as "advanced" on the SAT are not especially complex. Instead, they mostly use wording that is closer to what the writer of a professional natural science or social science article might employ.

Now, a prominent transition is NOT necessary for the first body paragraph. In fact, it is possible to just lead this one with an assertive topic statement. You may, however, use a transition if your first body paragraph features a VERY EARLY technique from the author's essay (paragraphs 1-2, for instance). Here are some acceptable transitions.

First Body Paragraph (Optional)

- "Initially,"
- "From the outset,"
- "To set a solid groundwork,"
- "In presenting [his/her] thesis,"
- "As an opening strategy,"

Transitions are much more necessary in the topic sentences of the second and third body paragraphs. Here, you need to show that your ideas cohere and interlock.

For these paragraphs, here are a few tried and true (and, frankly, easy to use) advanced vocabulary transitions.

Second and Third Body Paragraphs (Essential)

If you are simply moving to a new topic
- "Moreover,"
- "Furthermore,
- "In addition,"
- "Progressing further,"

If you are leading into a somewhat similar device
- "Similarly,"
- "Likewise,"
- "In a similar fashion,"
- "Using a complementary tactic,"

If you are leading into a very different device
- "Conversely,"
- "In a shift of tactics,"
- "Using a different strategy,"
- "Moving beyond such techniques"

Another effective though more subtle move is to situate a transition ("also," "moreover," "then") in the sentence itself—not at the opening:

- "The author then . . ."
- "The author, moreover, . . ."
- "The author's argument as a whole then . . ."

Such transitions are difficult to make noticeable, but they do indicate connectivity and may be appreciated as a sophisticated turn of sentence structure by some readers.

There is one further way to use transitions effectively, and to indicate that your ideas are well-coordinated in the process.

USE Cross-Reference Transitions

Here, you will craft transitions that briefly glance back at or "cross reference" what you have just talked about. For instance, imagine that you need connect these two paragraphs.

Body 1: linked examples

Body 2: cost-benefit analysis

You could use a transition such as the following to start Body Paragraph 2.

- "Beyond discussing linked examples, the author employs cost-benefit analysis . . . "

Such transitions can efficiently and intelligently show the reader how your essay moves along. However, two warnings are in order.

1) DO NOT over-use these. The PrepVantage template really only brings in ONE cross-reference transition, in part to create variety in sentence structure.

2) DO NOT run long with these. Mention each paragraph's main device early in your topic sentence (even if you cross-reference another device) and keep the transition itself to only a few words.

71

Chapter 7:
The Conclusion

Main Requirements

On recent SAT Essays, the conclusion has, admittedly, been treated as a minor element. At least this is the case where length is concerned. If you are used to writing long conclusions that restate all your important points, break that habit. NOW!

> ### Some recent high-scoring conclusions
> ### are ONLY TWO SENTENCES

You read that correctly. While the conclusion can be an important portion, it should NOT be a time-consuming portion. Your tasks in the conclusion are straightforward, yet are also designed to leave an excellent final impression on any readers who want EVERY paragraph to count.

Conclusion Requirements

1. Return to the Main Idea of the passage and continue to show comprehension
2. Provide a BRIEF synopsis of the techniques that appear in your body paragraphs
3. Continue to demonstrate variety and aptitude in sentence structure and vocabulary

There are a few ways to handle all of these tasks quickly and intelligently. You can deal with a basic structure that, to some extent, echoes the introduction of your essay.

Basic Conclusion Structure

Sentence 1. Statement indicating comprehension of Main Idea

Sentence 2: Statement relating Main Idea to author's devices

In practice, this is not a bad structure, but it can become somewhat choppy and mechanical unless you already have a fluent, well-connected writing style. For something more reliable—but that uses the same basic elements—consult the PrepVantage template that appears on the next page.

Important Tip: ALWAYS Write Some Sort of Conclusion

Realistically, you may end your third body paragraph with only a few minutes left. If so, still write AT LEAST one fairly developed sentence for the conclusion. Readers may question your knowledge of structure or your writing skill if you don't.

If you have this problem, though, don't let it persist. PRACTICE to perfect your timing.

Template

Sentence 1:

With his/her adept uses of rhetorical devices, [AUTHOR] affirms to his/her readers that [MAIN IDEA].

Sentence 2:

His/Her instances of [DEVICE 1], [DEVICE 2], and [DEVICE 3] are expertly designed to sway his/her audience, enabling readers to engage the issue of [TOPIC] in terms of both [CHOOSE: reasoning/evidence] and [CHOOSE: style/emotion/credible testimony].

You will notice that the template returns very directly to the ideas that you have already discussed. However, notice also that the two sentences do not break down rigidly. BOTH sentences discuss Main Idea and Devices. The conclusion offered by this template thus reads as a unified whole, a memorable, cogent response that rounds out the essay by bringing all of your most important ideas together.

After all, isn't that what a good conclusion should do?

Sample Conclusion

From the SAT Essay Response in Appendix B (Page 126-127)

With his adept uses of rhetorical devices, Sorelson affirms to his readers that self-driving technology is problematic. His instances of linked examples, direct address, and counter-arguments are expertly designed to sway his audience, enabling readers to engage the issue of self-driving cars in terms of both evidence and emotion.

Chapter 8:
Tricks and Traps

Basic Errors: Wording

You now have the fundamental structure of the entire SAT Essay. However, a good grasp of the main structure is NOT enough to guarantee you a high SAT Essay score. Instead, keep the following rule in mind.

> **you must EDIT AND PROOFREAD to satisfy even a quick reader**

The logic here is actually more straightforward than it may seem at first. A reader who only spends a few minutes with your SAT Essay submission will probably not pick up on nuanced shades of meaning (if you are used to writing essays that are deep and suggestive). But such a reader WILL see spelling and word choice flaws almost immediately, and has probably seen the SAME ONES repeatedly. Here are a few of the most common: the ones that you MUST avoid.

Major Misspellings

The absolute WORST misspelling on the SAT Essay is, in fact, linked to the main essay task itself.

arguement X   argument ✔

Students often misspell this because they are rushed, or because they think that the entire root "argue" needs to be preserved. WRONG. The word "argument" appears multiple times in the directions. If you get this spelling wrong, you may well be hit for committing a basic error on a word that is quite simple and is provided in its correct form anyway.

Other major misspellings to watch for, whether you are rushed or are just not accustomed to writing these words without spell-check, are the following.

definately X   definitely ✔

credebility X   credibility ✔

pursuade X   persuade ✔

commited X   committed ✔

responsable X   responsible ✔

examplification X   exemplification ✔

similie X   simile ✔

Watch ESPECIALLY for double consonants; it is very easy for students to rush right past these without even seeing the errors.

iresposible X   irresponsible ✔

In some cases, however, students will wrongly add double consonants to words that require single consonant combinations.

proffessional X   professional ✔

On a somewhat similar note, keep in mind that "ie" and "ei" combinations are very easy to get wrong. Particularly tricky here are the words that fall into the old "'i' before 'e' except after 'c' rule," a few of which are given below.

recieve X   receive ✔

acheive X   achieve ✔

Now, one or two spelling screw-ups will not destroy an otherwise effective five-paragraph essay. But because the SAT Reading and Writing sections do NOT really test spelling, it is easy for students to put spelling out of mind as a test criterion. The other sections do not matter here; keep your spellings correct and avoid the readers' wrath.

Author's Name and Gender

Seems simple, yes? However, even some very intelligent students assume that they can rush through these basics on their way to the analysis. If you consistently get information this obvious wrong, your essay will be populated with errors that distract the reader and that are liable to lower your Writing and possibly Reading scores.

For Name

There is really no excuse: consult ANY of the direction boxes. And make sure that you use both first and last name ONLY in the introduction. Afterwards, last name only will suffice in most cases.

For Gender

Consult the SECOND direction box. Some of the SAT Essay authors will have first names ("Dana," "Leslie," etc.) that could be either male or female. Fortunately, the PRONOUNS in this second box will give you the author's gender, without any question.

Keep in mind: one or two random mis-steps in these respects may not be catastrophic. But consistent flaws in these simple, straightforward areas will call your conscientiousness as a writer into question.

Subtle Errors: Ideas

Although there is a lot that can go wrong at the level of presentation and word choice, there can be much larger breakdowns in the SAT Essay. Many of these involve the presentation and coordination of ideas; all of them can be solved with a little pre-writing. Here are the main dangers to watch for.

Writing a Long Introduction or Conclusion X

Introductions and conclusions must remain short for a few reasons.

1) The body paragraphs are where you really demonstrate how the author's argument works, and should receive the most attention

2) The most recent high-scoring Official essay samples use VERY short introductions and conclusions

3) Long introductions and conclusions almost always contain "padding" and redundancies

Just stay with the length guidelines in Chapter 3 (Introduction) and Chapter 7 (Conclusion). Even if you have been taught to write longer introductions or conclusions in your English courses, DISREGARD those standards. In particular, do NOT recap every point you make in the conclusion. This can take anywhere from four to six sentences, and will chew up space that should be used for body paragraphs.

Also, remember, you are analyzing a 650- to 750-word essay, not an entire novel. While an English paper on a longer source justifies a fair amount of background and recapping, an analysis of such a short nonfiction passage does not.

Writing Almost Indistinguishable Body Paragraphs X

You have now examined how you can use some major topic areas (logic, credibility, style, emotion) to write an effective SAT Essay. However, you MUST make sure that your body paragraphs are distinct, ESPECIALLY if you are working within one of these topic areas multiple times. For instance, don't fall into the following trap:

Body Paragraph 1: Statistics ✔

Body Paragraph 2: Factual Evidence X

The problem here is evident upon examination: statistics ARE factual examples. In short, you will wind up with two body paragraphs that are virtually identical, or that read as much too close for comfort on a quick read.

To avoid this error, get in the habit of working with techniques that, on a quick read, are CLEARLY DIFFERENT. You can correct the problem above by analyzing to noticeably different types of logic.

Body Paragraph 1: Statistics ✔

Body Paragraph 2: Counter-Arguments ✔

Writing Two Over-Worked Body Paragraphs X

In other contexts, there may be plenty of justification for writing a very short, stunningly high-quality essay. The SAT Essay is not one of those contexts. You are dealing with very quick readers who will ASSUME that a student who writes more is a student who has more thoroughly analyzed the passage. It is up to you to deal with this assumption, even if you are accustomed to writing incredibly dense, incredibly concise prose.

Of course, we are not recommending that you write three mediocre body paragraphs and call it a day. But use your practice to get to three good body paragraphs under ANY conditions; never assume that your reader is reading closely enough to honor two absolutely brilliant body paragraphs with a top score. Few readers are.

About Logos, Pathos, and Ethos: A Few SAT Traps

You have may have noticed that we at PrepVantage avoid one of the major ways of analyzing the kind of argument-based passages that you will find in the SAT Essay. Logos, pathos, and ethos are three famous "rhetorical appeals": they are elements of how a convincing piece of persuasive writing or speech is constructed. And they can be loosely defined in the following manner.

Logos: Logic

Pathos: Emotion

Ethos: Credibility or Authority

The question, indeed, is what could go wrong with using these three clear concepts for three body paragraphs. Here are the major liabilities.

1) Name Dropping All Three Terms, Without Really Understanding Them

Remember, the SAT Essay tests how well you can analyze and explain an essay—NOT whether you possess advanced technical vocabulary. This is a "rhetorical analysis" essay, but you can write a perfect 24 without even knowing the term "rhetorical analysis." The same goes for logos, pathos, and ethos: you need to know how logic, emotion, and credibility WORK. What you call them is beside the point.

Unfortunately, some students think that specialized terminology will win over readers. Not really. Some recent high-achieving samples say NOTHING about logos, pathos, and ethos (at least not using those terms).

If these liabilities aren't enough, keep in mind that students who DO directly mention logos, pathos, and ethos often jam all three concepts together in the introduction—or, worse, in one of the three body paragraphs. The thesis will simply sound awkward; the body paragraph will try to address too many topics too quickly. This is bad organization, period.

2) Throwing Together Logos, Pathos, or Ethos Quotations Without Strong Connections

This is not the worst error you can commit, but it will hurt your ability to lock down 4s in Analysis. For each body paragraph, you need a central topic. Unfortunately, logos, pathos, and ethos are extremely broad categories and do NOT always lend themselves to coherent, centralized writing.

How does this happen? Consider logos: in any given essay, you may have several examples that broadly fit the category (factual examples, cause and effect, counter-arguments, analogies, solutions). Throwing together ALL of these in one paragraph will result in a jumbled piece of writing, and throwing together two or more without good connecting references may be just as bad.

The solution is simple: limit yourself to ONE or TWO major devices in each category. And if you do discuss multiple types of logos, pathos, or ethos in a single paragraph, make sure that those types are purposefully CONNECTED by your analysis.

3) Dealing with a Passage with Little or No Ethos

For logos, pathos, and ethos, the hardest one to find will often be ethos. You may see some excellent examples: if an author puts forward his or her accomplishments, background, or credentials, ethos can be quite obvious. However, ethos is, on average, the least-used of the three. In some of the College Board essays (particularly Practice Essay #3: "The Digital Parent Trap" by Eliana Dockterman), this quality does not appear in any readily apparent manner.

So don't expect a reliable ethos paragraph. You can of course double on logos or pathos (so long as you avoid the interchangeable paragraph trap described on page 81) Or, to pursue a different strategy, you can get comfortable with some of the less obvious forms of credibility, such as practical solutions or moral authority, as described in Chapter 4.

If, despite all this, you feel that you can still work with logos, pathos, and ethos effectively, go for it. Keep in mind that the tactics in this book map quite easily onto a logos, pathos, ethos arrangement, and do so in roughly the following manner.

Logos: Logic (Chapter 4)

Pathos: Style/Emotion (Chapter 5)

Ethos: Credibility (Chapter 4)

Chapter 9: Editing
Stronger Analysis

Avoiding Breakdowns in Paragraph Structure

Now that you have navigated around some of the fundamental essay errors, you can think about subscore-specific enhancements. The Analysis subscore, in particular, can be hard to lock down in a high scoring range. Fortunately, it is possible to address Analysis in a predictable manner and to avoid the most common Analysis liabilities—if you know what liabilities to look for.

In particular, Analysis can break down in terms of coordination WITHIN the individual paragraphs. These flaws come in a few major forms.

Over-Extended Body Paragraphs

As a rule, each body paragraph should be approximately EIGHT SENTENCES long. If you run significantly under, you will be dealing with under-developed analysis. Yet the dangers of writing an extremely long body paragraph are equally severe.

1) You will most likely wind up with one or two detrimentally short OTHER body paragraphs

2) You will probably begin combining too many topics or ideas in a poorly-coordinated manner

Problem 1 is not hard to foresee: your time, after all, is highly limited. Problem 2 is the more insidious threat, since you may be tempted to line up as many examples of a technique or tactic as you can—and may line up TOO MANY. That's if you know the PrepVantage strategies. If you DON'T, you will probably fall into the trap of throwing UNRELATED TOPICS into a single body paragraph.

SOLUTION: Be aggressive about streamlining your sentences AND your uses of evidence. Never put more than ONE TOPIC in a body paragraph, and never try for more than TWO MAJOR QUOTATIONS (perhaps with a few minor quoted terms).

Low-Quantity Analysis

Once you have figured out your body paragraph topics and quotations, you MUST make sure that you analyze the quoted materials at length. If you don't, you will wind up with an essay that reads like a group of quotations with lazy, ineffective connecting sentences.

You may, of course, excel at getting to the point of a quotation in a few short words. But SAT Essay quick readers REQUIRE volume; they want to see an essay that has quotations but that is still DOMINATED by your insights.

SOLUTION: Make sure to stay with roughly TWO important quotations per body paragraph, but make sure each one gets TWO SENTENCES of analysis. Treat this entirely as a matter of proportions.

Low-Precision Analysis

The other major breakdown results from now knowing WHAT to say about the quoted evidence. Your analysis must be well-directed and meaningful. In fact, it is rather easy to see when the analysis portions of a body paragraph are not meaningful: they usually lapse into vague value judgments such as the following:

"convincing" "effective" "authoritative" "persuasive"

Now, there is nothing wrong with using A FEW of these, since affirming that the author's stance is sensible will keep the essay on-topic. But if you have NOTHING more than vague words praising the author, you don't have analysis.

SOLUTION: Consult the PrepVantage charts to understand the SIGNIFICANCE of your chosen devices. (pages 40-44, 51-54, and 56-61.) These give you ways to talk about evidence WITHOUT delivering a series of interchangeable cliches.

Avoiding the "Summary Trap"

The last thing you want is an essay that reads as an extended summary of what you have just read. You may be able to lock down a decent Reading score with an essay that reads as a play-by-play recap of the passage; you will NOT, however, have a good chance at a strong Analysis score.

So how will you satisfy a quick reader? Keep in mind the tips about using quotations, and about spelling out the significance of the quotations that you have selected. Your solution will be straightforward if you do.

SOLUTION: DO NOT provide evidence exactly as it occurs in the passage. For example, avoid grouping quotations by body paragraph in the following manner

> Body 1: Paragraphs 1-3
>
> Body 2: Paragraphs 4-5
>
> Body 3: Paragraphs 6-9

and instead group body paragraphs BY TOPIC in the following manner.

> Body 1: Technique 1
>
> Body 2: Technique 2 . . .

If you organize your essay in this manner and make sure to incorporate STRONG TOPIC SENTENCES, you will naturally avoid the appearance of an extended summary.

Avoiding Generalities and "Padding" Sentences

Even the most advanced SAT Essay essay writers can lose sight of the passage at hand—and can lapse into broad and generalizing analysis of rhetorical or argumentative devices. This is NOT in any way a writing asset; instead, you need to keep your essay response focused on the passage.

In particular, writers are tempted to begin body paragraphs with general statements about how various writing techniques work.

Statistics help an author to establish credibility. X

Effective writing relies on emotional appeals. X

Statements such as these are simply padding: readers probably understand these concepts already, and should certainly get an idea of these concepts in the course of your analysis.

SOLUTION: Avoid generalized explanations of how rhetorical devices work, at ALL COSTS. Make sure, if you need to, that each topic sentence in some way refers to the following elements.

1) Author of Passage
2) Main Idea of Passage
3) Technique that you will analyze

The weak topic sentences above contain Element 3 only. Yet the strong topic sentence below contains all three.

By appealing to the emotion of fear, Sorelson devises a strong case against self-driving cars. ✔

Chapter 10: Editing
Stronger Writing Style

Enhancing the Vocabulary

One of the few problems with the predictability of the SAT Essay has to do with vocabulary. Because each essay assignment requires the same structure and the same kind of rhetorical analysis, you will necessarily return to the same few concepts on essay after essay. However, predictability or no predictability, you will STILL need to use vocabulary that is varied and impressive.

How can you pull this off? A good way to start is to know what words are most likely to be OVER-USED in any given SAT Essay response. Consult the next page for the repeat offenders in this respect.

Most Over-Used SAT Essay Words

Argument

Persuade

Builds (the argument)

States (verb)

As you can see, these words are all closely related to the nature of the essay task itself. You can't avoid them; however, you can't over-use "argument" or "persuades" until your reader's head spins, either.

The trick here is to find effective SYNONYMS for each word. On the next few pages, you will find charts that provide some of the most effective replacements for the four words listed above. Use our new word choices, but don't hesitate to add synonyms of your own.

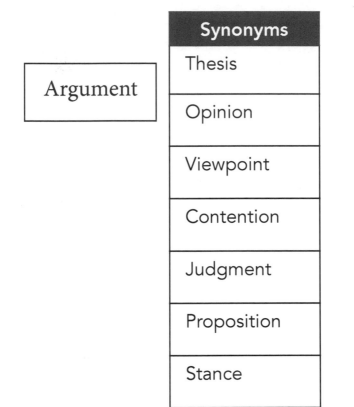

Argument	Synonyms
	Thesis
	Opinion
	Viewpoint
	Contention
	Judgment
	Proposition
	Stance

Synonyms of Your Own	

| Persuade |

Synonyms
Convince
Sway
Win Over
Instill
Compel
Induce
Lead

Synonyms of Your Own	

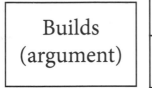

Builds (argument)

Synonyms
Develops
Substantiates
Constructs
Devises
Orchestrates
Crafts
Establishes

Synonyms of Your Own	

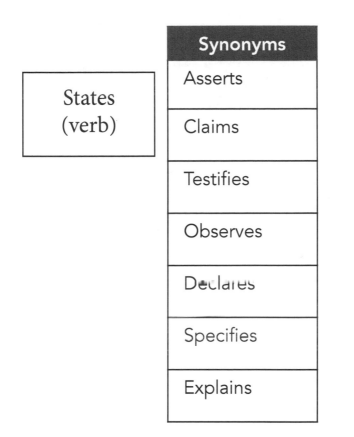

States (verb)	Synonyms
	Asserts
	Claims
	Testifies
	Observes
	Declares
	Specifies
	Explains

Synonyms of Your Own	

There are two other pieces of advice that you should keep in mind as you refine and enhance your use of vocabulary for the SAT Essay.

1) Continue to find synonyms for common concepts, including DEVICES and ADJECTIVES

The same principle that is at work in the charts that you have just seen should apply to future vocabulary work. Remember, SAT Essays are enormously predictable concept-wise. Your real challenge is to find new and impressive ways to phrase the same few concepts.

Here, you will want to work with synonyms in two areas. First, consider new ways of phrasing the DEVICES listed in Chapters 4 and 5. For instance, you may discuss "logic" quite prominently; just make sure to vary your wording while keeping your body paragraph coherent.

logic . . . reasoning . . . deduction . . . chain of ideas . . . argumentation . . . discourse . . . rationale

You will probably also find yourself returning to the same types of adjectives when describing the author's argument (positive) and possibly the author's opponents (negative). Here again, use synonyms. For example, you may find that you are emphasizing how "convincing" the author's ideas are. Don't worry about staying on one concept; just vary the wording.

convincing . . . compelling . . . effective . . . insightful . . . reliable . . . cogent . . . well-substantiated

The wording must be varied and somewhat advanced, but it MUST be case-appropriate, as the next piece of advice emphasizes

2) Be careful and make sure that your vocabulary is ADVANCED but NOT SHOWY

Vocabulary that is (relatively) advanced will impress readers. Nonetheless, your vocabulary for the SAT Essay does NOT need to comprise a large number of obscure words. In fact, if you try to bring in unusual or esoteric pieces of vocabulary, you may run the risk of mis-using them.

Here, consider the case of two words that are repeat offenders.

Both of these words mean "a very large number." Unfortunately, SAT Essay writers often misuse "myriad" or "plethora" (or both) to refer to only a few things ("the writer uses myriad reasons" when in fact the writer only uses three, etc.). An attentive reader will NOT be impressed.

But more importantly, the Re-designed SAT is NOT premised on extremely obscure vocabulary in any of its sections (Reading, Writing and Language, or the Essay). If you can use words that are appropriate but upper-level—not words that make you sound like an 18th century philosopher—you will do just fine.

Keep in mind also that not all synonyms are 100% interchangeable. As you study, learn the nuances of words that you intend to use and re-use.

Refining Sentence Structure

To make sure that you have an effective, varied, and mature style sentence-by-sentence, you should keep the following rules in mind.

1) Vary Sentence Openings

To make sure that your writing style is not monotonous, make sure that you vary the way you begin your sentences. The PrepVantage template (Appendix A) was designed with this rule as one of its premises. Yet if you want to rely a bit more on your own structure, a good rule to follow is the following.

- HALF of your sentences should feature simple declarative sentence or independent clause openings ("Sorelson claims that . . ."; "The article includes . . .")

- HALF of your sentences should open with transitions ("In contrast, . . ."; "Furthermore, . . .") or subordinate clauses ("Although these arguments seem valid . . ."; "Because he is indeed an expert . . .")

This variety is not hard to achieve, and is the first step towards creating impressively varied sentence structure overall. Moreover, repeated openings stand out, as in the following example.

Sorelson proves his point by employing information about his background. He explains that he is an investor in a company that "specializes in artificial intelligence for home use." He also shows that he has performed abundant research on the issue of self-driving cars.

The sentences are grammatically correct, but all open with simple noun-verb phrases. Try for more variety.

> In order to prove his point, Sorelson employs information about his background. He explains that he is an investor in a company that "specializes in artificial intelligence for home use." Moreover, he shows that he has performed abundant research on the issue of self-driving cars.

The changes are minimal, but the style has lost its repetitive quality.

Keep in mind that even writers who have very good command of sentence structure can lapse into repetition. High scoring writers, for instance, are liable to create too many sentence that begin with the following transitions.

By . . .   Because . . .   For instance/example, . . .

Here as well, the best way to avoid repetition is to revisit your work, diagnose your points of weakness, and use the guidelines above to refine your approach essay-by-essay.

2) Vary Sentence Length

Problems with sentence length are harder to spot on the fly than problems with sentence openings. But you can start to improve your style in this respect by keeping the following guideline in mind.

- OVERALL, you want a balance of relatively short (independent clause, possibly short transitions) and relatively long (subordinate clauses, long prepositional phrases, lists) sentences

It is somewhat difficult to find a rule of proportions here. However, if sentence length is a problem in your essays, you can figure out how to improve your style based on your particular weaknesses

Too Many Long Sentences

• Break up run-ons

• Add relevant short sentences for impact

Consider the following portion of a body paragraph, which crams too much information into one long and awkward sentence.

In discussing counter-arguments, Sorelson explains that Americans suffer "40,000 traffic fatalities" per year, a statistic that at first seems to support his opponents but is ultimately part of a larger strategy by which Sorelson presents himself as a balanced and credible source, one who can take a principled stand against the dangers of self-driving cars.

The grammar is technically correct, but the author's ideas appear to be thrown together—and will certainly be hard for a quick reader to sort out. Break up this sentence while achieving a diversity of sentence lengths and structures.

In discussing counter-arguments, Sorelson explains that Americans suffer "40,000 traffic fatalities" per year. This statistic at first seems to support his opponents, but is ultimately part of a larger strategy. Here, Sorelson presents himself as a balanced and credible source, one who can take a principled stand against the dangers of self-driving cars.

Now, consider the other sentence length liability

Too Many Short Sentences

• Combine judiciously while checking for grammar

• Check for structure and create better transitions

Sequences of short sentences are somewhat easier to catch: such portions often make for choppy reading and often (as an added weakness) feature sentences that follow extremely similar structures.

Tim Sorelson also appeals to the reader's sense of emotion. He conjures a positive future that may involve self-driving cars. Passengers will ride along, "sipping espresso and watching Seinfeld re-runs." Yet he wants the reader to realize that such a vision is a fantasy. Self-driving cars actually present an unrealistic vision of pleasure.

Again, the grammar is mostly correct, but these sentences show little skill in combining and connecting ideas. Just follow the combination and transition rules outlined above.

Tim Sorelson also appeals to the reader's sense of emotion by conjuring a positive future that may involve self-driving cars. Passengers will ride along, "sipping espresso and watching Seinfeld re-runs." Yet he wants the reader to realize that such a vision is a fantasy, since self-driving cars actually present an unrealistic vision of pleasure.

3) Watch for Construction and Grammar Flaws

There are a few standard grammar and construction flaws that you should watch for on the SAT Essay. Here are a few of the most problematic.

Redundant and Awkward Phrasing

As you introduce information, you must watch to make sure that you are doing so without creating unwieldy sentences with poor grammar. Often, SAT Essay test-takers will load simple sentences down with unnecessary words. One such flaw, in fact, occurs fairly regularly in introductions—with the first mention of the article.

> In "The Self-Driving Collision Course" by Tim Sorelson, the author explains . . . X

The wording here is already going wrong. There is no need to mention "Tim Sorelson" and then "the author," since the Sorelson IS the author. Eliminate this redundancy.

> In "The Self-Driving Collision Course," Tim Sorelson explains . . . ✓

As you re-read your practice essay responses, look for needlessly awkward and wordy constructions of this sort. Train yourself to eliminate them, and know the special cases (transitions to avoid comma splices, extra pronouns or phrases to avoid faulty comparisons) when additional phrasing can actually IMPROVE grammar.

Improper Use of Pronouns

Flaws in pronoun use come in a few forms. Watch, to begin, for confusions involving "IT" and "THEY."

"It" Usage

- Singular and CANNOT refer to a person

- Used to refer back to group-related nouns ("committee," "college," "government," "group") that are grammatically singular

It will always be wrong, for instance, to use the following constructions

> Early in the article, it states . . . X
> (since a person must "state")
>
> The country summoned their soldiers . . . X
> (since "country" is singular)

However, the following versions feature proper usage (or avoidance) of "it."

> Early in the article, the author states . . . ✔
>
> The country summoned its soldiers . . . ✔

"They" Usage

- Plural and refers to ALL plural nouns

- CANNOT refer to a singular person

In addition to avoiding "they" for certain collective yet singular nouns ("group," "assembly," "corporation," etc.), you must avoid using "they" to refer to ANY singular individual. This can be a tricky rule because it is frequently over-looked in everyday speech.

> . . . the author uses all of these devices to convince their audience . . . X ("their" refers to "author," singular)

> . . . each reader can easily see how the article's points relate to their life . . . X ("their" refers to "reader," singular)

Don't breeze past errors such as these on the SAT Essay. Just know that "author" can only take "his" or "her" references, and that "reader" should take the reference "his or her," or should be pluralized to "readers."

> . . . the author uses all of these devices to convince her audience . . . ✔

> . . . each reader can easily see how the article's points relate to his or her life . . . ✔

> . . . the readers can easily see how the article's points relate to their lives . . . ✔

Sentence Fragments

On the SAT Essay, sentence fragments—non-grammatical constructions that lack a main subject or a main verb—typically take one of two forms.

- Long, mostly-correct sentences with grammar breakdowns

- Short, poorly-worded phrases that are meant as references

Of these, the run-ons are somewhat harder to spot.

> With these quotations that highlight his use of strong emotion and speak to the reader's own desire for safety and security, Sorelson, indeed, who crafts a powerful rhetorical appeal. X

The sentence breaks down with the "who" transition, which prevents the sentence as a whole from ever taking on a true main clause. Watch for transitions such as this ("who," "which," "that") that create subordinate clauses, and for verbs that are turned into participles ("explaining") when they should function as main verbs ("explains"). All of these errors generate fragments.

Fortunately, these errors are easy to spot and fix, ESPECIALLY if you have time to proofread. Just check for a proper subject-verb combination. The rest of the sentence may be perfectly fine.

> With these quotations that highlight his use of strong emotion and speak to the reader's own desire for safety and security, Sorelson, indeed, crafts a powerful rhetorical appeal. ✔

Fragment errors can also arise from the usage of short and, frankly, sloppy phrases that are meant as quick explanations. These can occur in the vicinity of quotations.

> Sorelson stating that "[QUOTATION]" X

> "[QUOTATION]" Which indicates just how undesirable self-driving cars really are. X

Even if the ideas seem obvious, you CANNOT sacrifice grammar throughout the essay and expect a your scorer not to care. ALWAYS use full sentences.

> Sorelson states that "[QUOTATION]" ✔

> "[QUOTATION]" This evidence indicates just how undesirable self-driving cars really are. ✔

However, short phrases CAN sometimes help you to introduce quotations, as the next short section explains.

Working with Quotations

Use of quotations is a necessity on the SAT Essay. Though the readers will be looking primarily for how well you analyze your chosen quotations, there are a few rules of presentation to keep in mind.

1) Effective Transitions

Under NO circumstances should you avoid transitioning into a quotation. Although the College Board readers will know that your evidence and analysis are related, you need to demonstrate skill in simply presenting information.

Keep your transitions quick, though. Here are a few that allow you to present quotations with little difficulty.

Noun-Verb Phrases (with Comma)

"The author explains," "To make her case, the author declares," "Then, the author states,"

Noun-Verb Phrases (with "That")

"The final paragraph indicates that" "Ultimately, he concludes that" "These ideas lead into the author's idea that"

Quick Transition Phrases (FULL SENTENCE quotation, with Comma)

"As the author argues," "According to the final paragraphs,"

Note that only "THAT" constructions can operate without commas. Each of the other constructions listed should feature a single comma in order to set off the quotation; this is, in fact, a standard rule that is also tested in the SAT Writing section.

2) Discussing Quotations

After you have presented your quoted evidence, you MUST refer back to it in some way. Otherwise, a quick reader will be pressed to see how and where your evidence and analysis connect. Here are some phrases that you could use.

- As this quotation demonstrates, . . .

- Here, the author contends that . . .

- This evidence proves that . . .

You can also, once you have established this connectivity, quote VERY SMALL (one- to three-word) portions of the evidence that you have just set forward. Such miniature quotations help you to emphasize important concepts. Moreover, they show that you have found meaningful evidence that rewards sustained attention.

Ready to put your methods to the test?

Now that you have read through the full PrepVantage method, the next step is consistent practice with the SAT Essay.

As you work through sample essays, use the Checklist on the next page to make sure that your command of style and editing remains strong. Additional copies of the Checklist are available in Appendix D.

Writing Checklist

Does your essay successfully meet the following criteria in terms of writing style?

_____ Synonyms for over-used words

_____ Relatively advanced vocabulary

_____ Variety of sentence structures

_____ Differences in sentence length

_____ Proper transitions into quotations

_____ References back to quotations during analysis

_____ Few or no spelling and punctuation errors

Be completely honest about the state of your work, and consult the guidelines in this chapter as you read through. If you identify a weak point, focus on this area until you see clear improvement.

For additional copies of the Writing Checklist, please see Appendix D, pages 170-175.

Appendix A:

Complete Template
For the SAT Essay

This section of *10 Steps to the Perfect SAT Essay* contains a sentence-by-sentence outline for writing an exceptional SAT Essay submission. Though unified in its approach, the template can be used in any one of a few different ways, depending on your test-taking needs.

1. For extra guidance in drawing all the elements of the essay together, once you have finished Chapters 1-10

2. For testing out ideas and pairing the template recommendations against your own structure and style

3. For a crash course in writing the essay, with little other preparation or strategy

If you are pressed for time, you can definitely try the third of these approaches. It may give you better results than going in and taking the essay without any other reading; however, as you will see, you will need strategies from elsewhere in this book to make the template work at its absolute best.

The first paragraph of the template will, naturally, be the introduction. For now we are keeping this short, since high-scoring recent essays often used four sentences (and sometimes far fewer) to earn perfect and near-perfect scores.

INTRODUCTION

As [AUTHOR] demonstrates in "[TITLE]," [FIRST STATEMENT FROM MAIN IDEA]. However, the significance of [AUTHOR]'s chosen issue does not end there; for him/her, [SECOND STATEMENT FROM MAIN IDEA]. [AUTHOR] effectively establishes and substantiates his/her argument about [MAIN IDEA] by employing [DEVICE 1], by using [DEVICE 2], and by presenting [DEVICE 3].

NOTES

For Main Idea: See Chapter 2 (Pages 18-25)

For Devices: See Chapters 4 (Pages 36-45) and 5 (Pages 46-62)

Please keep in mind that FIRST reference to the author should list both first and last name. Except in circumstances (or if you need to repeat first and last name for emphasis in the conclusion), this will be the ONLY usage of both first and last name for the author of the passage.

FIRST BODY PARAGRAPH

[AUTHOR] crafts a [adj. describing DEVICE 1] argument by incorporating [DEVICE 1] that illuminates his/her main topic: [TOPIC FROM MAIN IDEA]. In the course of his/her discussion, he/she asserts that "[QUOTATION 1, DEVICE 1]." This information is intended to show the reader [SIGNIFICANCE, Q1D1], and to do so in a manner that [SIGNIFICANCE, Q1D1]. On account of [AUTHOR]'s evidence, readers can understand that [SIGNIFICANCE, Q1D1]. Yet [AUTHOR]'s use of [DEVICE 1] does not stop here; he/she continues on to explain that "[QUOTATION 2, DEVICE 1]." With such a quotation, [AUTHOR] expands his/her thesis outward to assert that [SIGNIFICANCE, Q2D1]. The true significance of such information is that it shows [SIGNIFICANCE, Q2D1].

NOTES

For Significance: See the charts (Pages 40-44, 51-54, and 56-61.)

SECOND BODY PARAGRAPH

Beyond articulating his/her ideas using [DEVICE 1],
[AUTHOR] also employs [evidence/reasoning/
language] that is perfect for [DEVICE 2,
EXPLANATION]. For instance, [AUTHOR] states
that "[QUOTATION 1, DEVICE 2]." As an author,
he/she is attuned to [SIGNIFICANCE, Q1D2]. Yet
[AUTHOR] later puts [DEVICE 2]
to another use, "[QUOTATION 2, DEVICE 2]."
With this quotation, [AUTHOR] moves from
[SIGNIFICANCE, Q1D2] to the new tactic of
[SIGNIFICANCE, Q2D2]. Here, he/she appeals to
[SIGNIFICANCE, Q2D2].

THIRD BODY PARAGRAPH

[AUTHOR]'s writing is also guided by another especially potent tactic, the use of [DEVICE 3]. As [AUTHOR] explains: "[QUOTATION 1, DEVICE 3]." This [adj. describing Q1D3] statement helps [AUTHOR] to establish [SIGNIFICANCE, Q1D3]. Building on this important sentence, [AUTHOR] then explains that "[QUOTATION 2, DEVICE 3]." [AUTHOR], on the basis of this evidence, is no [FALSE CHARACTERIZATION OF AUTHOR]. Instead, he/she proves through information of this sort that he/she is [TRUE CHARACTERIZATION OF AUTHOR]; he/she is well aware of [SIGNIFICANCE, Q2D3].

CONCLUSION

With his/her adept uses of rhetorical devices, [AUTHOR] affirms to his/her readers that [MAIN IDEA]. His/Her instances of [DEVICE 1], [DEVICE 2], and [DEVICE 3] are expertly designed to sway his/her audience, enabling readers to engage the issue of [TOPIC] in terms of both [reasoning/evidence] and [style/emotion/credible testimony].

Want to see exactly how the template works?

For an example of an essay that follows the template, take some time to read over the high-scoring sample essay on pages 123-127. You will notice that some elements of the template are used word-for-word. However, do not assume that this is the only way to respond to the template. If you need to modify it slightly for a "personalized" template of your own, go for it!

Appendix B:

Sample Essay
For the Full Strategy

How to Use This Section

If you have consulted the individual chapters and Appendix A, perhaps you have already seen how to use the complete SAT Essay template. However, to fully appreciate how this template works, you should see how it quickly generates a powerful essay.

In this appendix, you will be given a sample of the essay that is referenced throughout the book: "The Self-Driving Collision Course" by Tim Sorelson. You will then see how the PrepVantage template can be used to take the core information from this essay as the basis of an excellent student response.

This section can be a crash course in how to write an effective single submission. But perhaps this appendix is better taken as a first step towards your own concentrated practice—which will be facilitated with the five up-to-date essays in Appendix C.

Essay Begins on the Next Page

Practice Essay: Sample

Adapted from Tim Sorelson, "The Self-Driving Collision Course." May 27, 2017. Copyright PrepVantage Publishing.

1 As a skeptic of self-driving cars, I can find myself in the company of some unappealing lines of thought. The reasons for making most cars autonomous—and, by so doing, removing a lot of human error from a high-risk activity—can after all sound fairly compelling. Such vehicles could prevent or at least trim down the 40,000 traffic collision fatalities that occur on American roads every year. They could be a step towards developing new robotics, artificial intelligence, and clean energy technologies. They would give you time to read a book or watch old *Seinfeld* reruns instead of staring at the road and stewing in frustration during that 45-minute commute. What's not to love about a car that doubles as your personal chauffeur?

2 And what's not to hate about some of the attacks that are brought *against* self-driving cars? To oppose these vehicles is, so it appears, to stand squarely against the technology of the future. Just as bad as being on the wrong side of history is the prospect of being on the wrong side of some current-day disputes. There is a strong likelihood that self-driving cars would also utilize some hybrid or electric car technology; this approach would easily eat into the revenues of the environmentally- and geopolitically- maligned oil and gas industries. With fewer accidents to file lawsuits over, personal injury lawyers would naturally see their earnings suffer as well.

3 Yet self-driving cars wouldn't only hurt pollution-happy oil tycoons and shady attorneys. There is much more that could

go wrong in a self-driving future, starting with your basic commute home.

4 The first thing to consider is that self-driving technology won't be able to do everything, at least not in the first several years of its adoption; realistically, it will require the active and consistent oversight of the driver. We already have a model for what such not-quite-self-driving technology looks like in the Tesla Model PTS-D, a luxury car that uses some self-driving functions to assist in parking and to avoid the worst collisions.

5 So self-driving cars will not by any means completely "take over" the driving process. They won't even be able to take over what they are supposed to take over without glitches: the Tesla model just mentioned was at the center of a 2016 controversy, in which a Tesla on "autopilot" crashed into another car. Nor are self-driving cars, as currently conceived, particularly good at addressing conditions such as rain or snow. In fact, the human driver who knows the weird patterns of flooding near his or her home is probably better at dealing with heavy weather than any computer algorithm.

6 Still, where self-driving cars may genuinely excel is in dealing with traffic patterns, especially if there is a critical mass of other self-driving cars—vehicles that can use A.I. to efficiently network with one another—on the road. This is a fascinating prospect: a synchronized legion of self-driving vehicles, turning and passing and weaving effortlessly. Yet it is, for all its futuristic thrill, an unlikely prospect.

7 Creating a world of self-driving cars will require massive resources, though not resources that are beyond the reach of today's mightiest corporations. The problem, really, is that no existing corporation could manage a wide-scale transition to self-driving technology. Google created self-

driving car prototypes but didn't get much beyond that; though a fantastically inventive company in terms of marketing and web products, Google doesn't create much in the way of innovative physical products, and what few it has created (hello, Google Glass) haven't gone anywhere. The other companies that could lead a self-driving revolution may have even greater liabilities. Tesla creates mostly high-end vehicles, not mass-market technology; the ride-hailing service Uber has long gravitated to self-driving cars, but has been mired in corporate scandal for the past two years.

8 I bring up these criticisms not as a Luddite*, but as a board member in a company that specializes in artificial intelligence for home use. If my own colleagues were to propose an investment in self-driving technology, I would oppose them in a heartbeat. As of now, the drawbacks are too clear, the industry leadership too weak. One day, perhaps, we will all make our way home in self-driving pods, sipping espresso and letting the on-board computer deal with every mean curve and nasty intersection. But that day will not be today, or tomorrow, or any day long, long after.

*Luddite: one who is opposed to technological progress in a narrow or reactionary manner.

Write an essay in which you explain how Tim Sorelson builds an argument to persuade his audience that the widespread adoption of self-driving cars would be counterproductive. In your essay, analyze how Sorelson uses one or more of the features listed in the box above (or features of your own choice) to strengthen the logic and persuasiveness of his argument. Be sure that your analysis focuses on the most relevant features of the passage.

Your essay should not explain whether you agree with Sorelson's claims, but rather explain how Sorelson builds an argument to persuade his audience.

High-Scoring Response: 4/4/4

As Tim Sorelson demonstrates in "The Self-Driving Collision Course," adopting self-driving cars as a new norm in modern transportation would create major problems for consumers and companies. However, the significance of Sorelson's chosen issue does not end there; for him, the reality that self-driving cars are counterproductive contradicts common fantasies about these vehicles. Sorelson effectively establishes and substantiates his argument against self-driving car usage by employing case studies about major companies, by using direct address, and by presenting the faulty counter-arguments of his opponents.

Sorelson crafts a rigorous argument by incorporating business-world evidence that illuminates his main topic: self-driving cars are inadvisable. In the course of his discussion, he asserts that one self-driving

"Tesla model . . . was at the center of a 2016 controversy, in which a Tesla on 'autopilot' crashed into another car." This information is intended to show the reader that self-driving technology is fundamentally dangerous, and to do so in a manner that portrays Sorelson as a knowledgeable commentator. On account of Sorelson's evidence, readers can understand that even prestigious corporations cannot master self-driving technology. Yet Sorelson's use of linked examples does not stop here; he continues on to explain that other leading self-driving companies are Google and Uber, "which has been mired in corporate scandal for years." With such a quotation, Sorelson expands his thesis outward to assert that Tesla is not alone in mis-managing self-driving cars. The true significance of such information is that it shows how difficult it will be to responsibly create self-driving vehicles, even when companies with vast resources are involved.

Beyond articulating his ideas using linked examples, Sorelson also employs direct address language that is perfect for connecting to his reader. For instance, Sorelson asks, "What's not to love in a car that doubles as your personal chauffeur?" As an author, he is attuned to his reader's desires and emotions. Yet Sorelson later puts approachable language to another use, stating "There is much that could go wrong with a self-driving future, starting with your basic commute home." With this quotation, Sorelson moves from simply connecting to the reader to the new tactic of challenging the reader's assumptions. Here, he indicates that there are everyday, fear-inducing problems that self-driving cars will involve.

Sorelson's writing is also guided by another especially potent tactic, the use of refuted counter-arguments. As Sorelson explains, self-driving car opponents appear to be "on the wrong side" of the issue. This blunt statement helps Sorelson to establish his own awareness of the opposition that he faces Building on this important idea, Sorelson then further establishes credibility: he references his professional expertise and explains that "If my own colleagues were to propose an investment in self-driving technology, I would oppose them in a heartbeat." Sorelson, on the basis of this evidence, is no uninterested observer. Instead, he proves through information of this sort that he is both conscientious and assertive; he is well aware of the other side of the issue yet determined to maintain his stance in a manner that wins the reader's admiration.

With his adept uses of rhetorical devices, Sorelson affirms to his readers that self-driving technology is problematic. His instances of linked examples, direct address, and counter-arguments are expertly designed to sway his audience, enabling readers to engage the issue of self-driving cars in terms of both evidence and emotion.

Essay Scoring: 4/4/4 (One Reader)

As you can see, the PrepVantage template provides several benefits: consistent quotation usage, orderly transitions, insightful yet efficient introduction and conclusion. Here are some other strengths of the essay that you have just seen, as broken down by sub-score.

Reading, 4: Throughout, the writer expresses insightful comprehension of the problems with self-driving cars, according to Sorelson. The introduction, for instance, moves beyond the statement in the box: self-driving technology hurts both "companies and consumer" and is linked to flawed "fantasies" Both the introduction and conclusion call attention to the passage's most important points and main rhetorical devices, setting up coherent body paragraphs.

Analysis, 4: In each body paragraph, the writer focuses on a single device (linked examples, second-person direct address, counter-arguments) and clearly explains its significance. All observations clearly show how the thesis in the passage is articulated and supported, whether through logic, credibility, style, or emotion. Quotations are kept concise and clearly fit the paragraph topics. Note that the writer does modify some of the template wording from Appendix A: you SHOULD do make such modifications if you need to accommodate an important quotation using a different sentence structure.

Writing, 4: While the template from Appendix A ensures effective transitions and a varied, mature style, the writer also brings in appropriate and effectively varied upper-level vocabulary ("inadvisable," "commentator," "conscientious and assertive"). There are no major breakdowns in the movement from idea to idea, and no noticeable flaws in spelling, grammar, or diction.

To further understand the strengths of the essay above, consider the flaws that occur in weaker essays on the same topic. Here are two essays that (while not terrible enough to be stuck only with 1 or 2 subscores) are nonetheless burdened by exactly the weaknesses that the PrepVantage method is designed to address.

Low-Scoring Response 1:

In "The Self-Driving Collision Course" by Tim Sorelson, the author builds an arguement to persuade his audience that the widespread adoption of self-driving cars would be counterprodductive. He uses evidence, reasoning and stylistic or emotional appeals to build his arguement.

Tim Sorelson uses evidence to argue that self-driving cars are counterprodductive.

In paragraph 1 it states "Such vehicles could prevent or at least trim down the 40,000 traffic collission fatalities that occur on American roads every year." He uses this evidence to show that self-driving cars are dangerous because they would only cause more collissions. Instead of making people safer more collissions would happen because of self-driving cars.

Tim also uses logical reasoning to make his arguement. In paragraph 5 it states "self-driving cars will not by any means completely "take over" the driving process. They won't even be able to take over what they are supposed to take over without glitches." Because self-driving cars will have glitches they will not be useful techology that the reader should want. Because they are unsafe, readers can see from Tim Sorelson that self-drivng cars are counterprodductive.

Tim Sorelson uses lastly stylistic or

persuasive elements, such as word choice or appeals to emotion. In paragraph 8 it states "One day, perhaps, we will all make our way home in self-driving pods, sipping espresso and letting the onboard computer deal with every mean curve and nasty intersection." By stating this, Tim wants the reader to see that self-driving cars are the technology of the future and are still counterprodductive. He also uses a call-to-arms appeal with "we" to show that we should all see the problems with self-driving cars and support the author's arguement.

In conclusion, in "The Self-Driving Collision Course" Tim Sorelson builds an argument to persuade his audience using evidence, reasoing and stylistic or emotional appeals to build his arguement.

Essay Scoring: 2/3/2 (One Reader)

In terms of structure, this essay does meet the expected five paragraphs and does incorporate important quotations. However, even a quick reader will be able to see some major deficiencies; these are outlined in the scoring breakdown below.

Reading, 2: This essay demonstrates awareness of the main idea that appears in the directions box towards the end of the essay. However, the writer's comprehension of the essay's main premise does not extend much beyond the idea that self-driving cars are negative and dangerous. A less exacting reader, or one who is more forgiving of repetition of the directions, would probably give a Reading score of 3.

Analysis, 3: The writer understands the analytical task and identifies a few important devices. Weaknesses arise, though, because the writer's analysis seldom ties evidence back to the main idea in a nuanced or insightful manner. (Note also that the writer completely mis-reads the quotation presented in the first body paragraph.) Additional quotations are also needed for development of the strongest possible body paragraphs. A reader who is attentive to the fine points of close reading of evidence would probably give an Analysis score of 2.

Writing, 2: Overall, this writer's submission is burdened by misspellings, repetition of phrases taken straight from the directions, and awkward, repeating sentence structure. These significant weaknesses in style and vocabulary work against the reasonably coherent paragraph structure.

Keep in mind that what you have just read is, despite its many flaws, a five-paragraph essay. A breakdown in essay structure can also occur on the SAT Essay. To understand a different set of problems, consider the following, very different low-scoring response.

Low-Scoring Response 2:

With a myriad of creative writing techniques, a writer can persuade an audience that his idea is correct and powerful in its intent. In Tim Sorelson's article "The Self Driving Collision Course," Sorelson is compelling in persuading his audience that there are definite problems with the self-driving cars that all of expect to oneday emerge as a common technology. He uses ethos, pathos, and logos appeals. With these arguments Sorelson, indeed, creates a case that will have readers nodding their heads in agreeance with his man ideas about the problems with self-driving cars and their acceptance.

Logos and ethos help a writer to both

establish strong logic and to prove his or her credibility to the reader. For instance, Sorelson uses a strong logical rhetorical appeal when he states "there is much more that could go wrong with self-driving cars." (Sorelson, paragraph 4) With logic such as we see here, Sorelson builds his comprehension of how self-driving cars are problematic, so that the audience will understand the logic and statistics that can be used to disprove the arguments in favor of self-driving cars. Self-driving cars, after all cause traffic fatalities on the basis of evidence from companies such as Tesla and Google. The combination of pathos and ethos in Sorelson's article is also important, since pathos and ethos enable the reader to see that an author is both emotional and credible. Sorelson tells us he is "a board member of a company that specializes in artificial intelligenc." (Sorelson, paragraph 8) This quotation shows us that Sorelson is an expert in the issue that he has chosen to discuss, and pulls us onto Sameulson's side becuase of this. The quotatin is also proof that Sorelson has an emotional urgency when talking about self-driving cars, although some readers may think from earlier paragraphs that he is just a journalist giving specific data and statistics about the problem.

Overall, Sorelson uses ethos, pathos, and logos along with statistics and rhetorical questions to help the reader understand that self-driving cars are going to hurt society if we are foolish enough to adopt them

Essay Scoring: 3/2/3 (One Reader)

For a quick reader, the most significant problem may be that the analysis is mostly jammed together in one extremely large body paragraph. However, there are other flaws that stand out in this essay.

Reading, 3: The writer does seem to grasp the main idea that self-driving cars are an increasingly intriguing yet extremely problematic technology, and provides a few main reasons for the passage's overall negative stance. Yet because the writer relies on confusing transitions and overly general statements, proof of more nuanced comprehension is hard to locate in the body of the essay.

Analysis, 2: In this response, the analysis (the one large body paragraph) is a collection of ideas that are hard to separate out. Logos, pathos, and ethos are mentioned but are treated superficially. Moreover, the writer is over-reliant on paraphrasing and includes only a few quotations, most of which are passed by without sustained attention.

Writing, 3: Sentence-by-sentence, the writing is mostly free of glaring and distracting errors, and the writer does have some command of fairly advanced vocabulary. However, there are flaws in grammar, run-on sentences, needless generalities, and some made-up words. These problems would not be enough to justify a lower score on their own. Keep in mind, though, that a reader who expects more orderly work with paragraph-by-paragraph organization may give a Writing score of 2.

Now that you have seen these weaknesses in action, you can consult the next segment--Appendix C--for sample further sample prompts and sample responses. From now on, you will be dealing only with high-scoring material. Keep learning from the best.

Appendix C:

Four New Essays
Additional Practice

How to Use This Section

Now that you have worked through the full PrepVantage strategy, you will need reliable practice material for SAT Essay success. For that purpose, you can begin with the five essays gathered here. These passages offer a few unique advantages.

1. Reflect the topics and structure of the most recent College Board essay passages

2. Feature uniquely challenging versions of standard SAT Essay devices and writing structures

3. High-scoring responses and techniques for each essay posted at prepvantagebooks.com/essay

As you practice, try to intersperse these passages with the College Board selections. You might want to consult the most recent Official releases as your test day nears, but the varied and challenging PrepVantage essay prompts can set the best possible groundwork for an excellent score.

Practice Essay #1

Adapted from Christine Lehr. "A Museum Is Not a Soft Drink: Misadventures in Brand Identity" Copyright PrepVantage Publishing (December 2017).

1 One of the most blazingly foolish decisions on the history of modern museums had nothing to do with a work of art, an artist, or an exhibition. Well, not directly. The uproar this time—as much uproar as we arts-and-culture types are inclined to make, at least—surrounded the logo of the Metropolitan Museum of Art. That logo, until 2016, was a stately "M," its proportions determined by an efficient network of lines and circles appropriate to an architectural blueprint. But the "M" wasn't truly "architectural": its real backstory is that it was transposed almost line-for-line from a manuscript by Fra Luca Pacioli, a pupil of Leonardo Da Vinci and an adherent—like his famed Renaissance mentor—of a classical sense of form and order.

2 So it was from 1971 (the "M" debut) to 2016 (the debut of the new logo, such as it was). Today, the Met bears a logo that has next to nothing to do with that Da Vinci-esque "M." The current logo was designed not by a virtuoso artist, but by branding and consulting firm Wolff Olins. It consists of two sort-of words—"THE MET"—executed in red serif letters that seem, for lack of a better phrases, smushed together. Architecture critic Justin Davidson has dubbed it a "typographic bus crash." To me, it looks more like someone who doesn't know a single letter of Russian had attempted to write his name in Russian, and using ketchup.

3 But why does anyone care about this? It is one logo for one museum, and as you can see above it's giving us arts-and-culture types fun fodder for snarky comments. Well, snark aside, we do care. The world of art, museums, and yes logos must open itself to inevitable change, yet the institutions that we rely on have a funny habit of betraying the one rule that any decent doctor knows to follow: "First, do no harm."

4 Who is harmed by a change of logo, though? Only the people who care of course: people whose energies are better spent promoting the arts than writing outraged commentaries like Davidson's (and mine) in the hopes that museums will wise up and correct their lapses in taste. And yet these miniature controversies sap precious energies every few years. The Whitney Museum faced its own flurry of angry comments when it changed its logo—from blocky "WHITNEY" lettering to slightly less blocky "WHITNEY" lettering accompanied by a giant, geometric W—back in 2013. This is not the art world discussion we need to be having, with attendance at museums (like the Met) continuing to drop, with budget cuts to high school programs in the arts. But we are having it. The museums made us do it.

5 And museums don't act like museums anymore; they act more like corporations. The fact that a museum needs to periodically "refresh" its brand—almost like Microsoft changing the angle of its Windows logo or Google re-working the font of its search engine text—is not a good sign, not at all. It's a terrible sign: are museums there to house the finest in human culture, or to play to whatever draws an audience? Another, the Museum of Modern Art, hasn't gutted its logo just yet. But it has re-designed its once intimate premises to create a big, airy, "corporate" building—perfect for bringing "installations" by Internet celebrities and pop singers front and center, while the paintings and sculptures and classic films hide out somewhere upstairs.

6 Ironically, re-branding this major usually doesn't work. Coke tried a "New Coke" beverage that its Coke loyalists hated; RadioShack rebranded as "The Shack" on the way to watching its market share disappear. Branding failures such as these are simply unfortunate, but when a museum starts tweaking its brand it actually starts to erase parts of its history. These places are the repositories of history, culture, and art after all, and the wrong choice can jumble and distort and cheapen that network of achievements and memories— not enhance it. In the case of the Met, re-branding destroyed the rare logo that was itself a work of art. Harm done.

Write an essay in which you explain how Christine Lehr builds an argument to persuade her audience that museums should not change their logos and identities. In your essay, analyze how Lehr uses one or more of the features listed in the box above (or features of your own choice) to strengthen the logic and persuasiveness of her argument. Be sure that your analysis focuses on the most relevant features of the passage.

Your essay should not explain whether you agree with Lehr's claims, but rather explain how Lehr builds an argument to persuade her audience.

High-Scoring Response: 4/4/4

As Christine Lehr demonstrates in "A Museum Is Not a Soft Drink," museums that seek to re-construe their identities pursue a fundamentally flawed approach. However, the significance of Lehr's chosen issue does not end there; for her, supposedly re-invented museums only alienate once-loyal visitors through logo, marketing, and identity changes. Lehr effectively establishes and substantiates her argument about problems with museum re-branding by analyzing repercussions and consequences, by using stark visual descriptions, and by presenting her ideas in a tone of urgency and involved concern.

Lehr crafts a lucid argument by incorporating analysis of repercussions that illuminates her main topic: the counter-productive effects of altering a museum's identity. In the course of her discussion of museum re-branding efforts, she asserts that such "miniature controversies sap precious energies every few years." This information is intended to show the reader that the effects of changing even a single logo are unexpectedly significant, and to do so in a manner that calls attention to the manner in which such logos distract well-meaning commentators. On account of Lehr's evidence, readers can understand that problems in "museum attendance" and "budget cuts" go unaddressed as a result of logo disputes. Yet Lehr's use of consequence-based analysis does not stop here; she continues on to explain that the "wrong choice [of logo] can jumble and distort and cheapen that network of achievements and memories—not enhance it.." With such a quotation, Lehr expands her thesis outward to assert that one clear consequence of re-branding is self-inflicted harm to an institution. The true significance of such information is that it shows the array of consequences—for students, commentators, and museum—that poor logo choices inflict.

Beyond articulating her ideas using repercussion-based reasoning, Lehr also employs language that is perfect for creating powerful visual contrasts. For instance, Lehr states that the original, exceptional Metropolitan Museum logo was formed from "an efficient network of lines and circles appropriate to an architectural blueprint." As an author, she is attuned to her reader's need to create firm mental pictures of the very logos that she admires for their beauty. Yet Lehr later puts visual imagery to another use, critically describing the replacement logo as something that looks "like someone who doesn't know a single letter of Russian had attempted to write his name in Russian, and using ketchup." With this part of her passage, Lehr moves from praising one of the vanished beauties of museum branding to the new tactic of visually capturing the tacky, ridiculous nature of museum re-branding. Here, she appeals to the reader's visual imagination, helping her audience to envision and loathe the re-branding efforts that she herself despises.

Lehr's writing is also guided by another especially potent tactic, the use of an urgent and engaged tone. As Lehr explains, identity alteration by institutions such as the Museum of Modern Art and the Whitney is not a good sign, not at all. It's a terrible sign." This blunt statement helps Lehr to establish her visceral, passionate investment in her chosen issue. Building on this important content, Lehr then explains that re-branding at the Met "destroyed the rare logo that was itself a work of art. Harm done." Lehr, on the basis of this evidence, is no detached and dryly academic "art world" commentator. Instead, she proves through information of this sort that she is eager to transmit her sense of concern and urgency to the reader; she is well aware that she must win her audience by showing that she has chosen an emotionally charged issue.

With her adept uses of rhetorical devices, Lehr affirms to her readers that changing museums' identities is an ill-advised approach. Her instances of repercussions, descriptive language, and personal concern are expertly designed to sway her audience, enabling readers to engage the issue of museum re-branding in terms of both firm reasoning and elegant writing style.

Continue reading for more Essays

Practice Essay #2

**Adapted from U.S. Senator Lisa Murkowski.
Introduction of Bipartisan Sportsmen's Act of 2015.
Delivered to the Senate on Febuary 5, 2015.**

1 We are here today not just to announce the re-introduction of our Bipartisan Sportsmen's Act, but also to renew the conversation about its importance—and to urge the Senate to come together to prioritize its passage.

2 Our sportsmen and women come from all over the country, from big cities and small towns, from the north and the south. For many of us, outdoor activities are a tradition that is passed down from generation to generation. Hunting and fishing are best-known among them, but the enthusiasts who go outside to boat or recreationally shoot enjoy a long tradition as well.

3 Sportsmen and women also play an important role in our economy. In 2013, approximately 37 million people hunted or fished in America. That is roughly equal to the population of California, and those numbers are always increasing.

4 With these impressive numbers comes a huge economic impact. Sportsmen and women spent roughly $90 billion in 2013, and those numbers have likely risen since then. Their dollars go not only to gear and equipment, but also to the travel industry, to the hospitality industry, and to many other sectors of our economy.

5 Spending by sportsmen and women also aids conservation efforts. Excise taxes on fishing, hunting, and shooting equipment, motorboat fuel, as well as fees for licenses and stamps, are all dedicated to state fish and wildlife

management and conservation. These individuals care deeply for the environment and for conservation, which is why these excise taxes are in place to take care of our natural resources. Since their establishment, the Wildlife and Sport Fish Restoration programs have contributed over $14.5 billion to conservation.

6 Turning to my home State for a moment, in Alaska alone there are over 125,000 individuals who engage in hunting each year. This in turn has created more than $439 million in retail sales and $195 million in salaries and wages. Hunting in Alaska also brings in over $53 million to State and local governments each year. . .

7 Our Bipartisan Sportsmen's Act of 2015 builds on last year's effort, which was broadly supported by 46 members of this chamber. . . I want to take a few moments to discuss provisions in this package that are especially important from my perspective.

8 First is a bill that I have championed for several years, the Recreational Fishing and Hunting Heritage and Opportunities Act. It protects recreational hunting and fishing on Bureau of Land Management and National Forest lands while reaffirming other prior Congressional actions enacted to protect hunting and wildlife conservation.

9 My bill—again in this year's broader package—requires that BLM and Forest Service land be open to hunting, recreational fishing, or recreational shooting as a matter of law unless the managing agency acts to close lands to such activities. Leaving lands open unless closed means that agencies need not take action to open them to hunting and fishing. The agencies are still permitted to close or place restrictions on land for a number of purposes, including resource conservation and public safety. But on the whole,

147

this is an affirmation that sportsmen and women are welcome on America's public lands.

10 Next, I would like to discuss the Hunting, Fishing, and Recreational Shooting Protection Act—which has again been included. This bipartisan provision was previously introduced by Senators Thune and Klobuchar as a standalone bill. Its language is very important to many of us and to nearly all of the sportsmen's groups that we have heard from.

11 This provision is necessary to push back against some extreme environmental groups who have been attempting to ban all traditional ammunition under the Toxic Substances Control Act. Their attack has reinforced the need for Congress to preserve and protect the rights of all sportsmen to choose their own ammunition and fishing tackle. As many of us know, traditional ammunition and fishing tackle are significantly less expensive than alternative options, so this provision could quite literally be the difference in whether many sportsmen and women are able to continue participating in outdoor activities.

12 . . . As we move this bipartisan effort along, I strongly encourage all of our colleagues, on both sides of the aisle, to support the thousands of sportsmen and women in their home states by joining us in cosponsoring this important legislation.

Write an essay in which you explain how Lisa Murkowski builds an argument to persuade her audience that the activities of sportsmen should receive legislative promotion and protection. In your essay, analyze how Murkowski uses one or more of the features listed in the box above (or features of your own choice) to strengthen the logic and persuasiveness of her argument. Be sure that your analysis focuses on the most relevant features of the passage.

Your essay should not explain whether you agree with Murkowski's claims, but rather explain how Murkowski builds an argument to persuade her audience.

High-Scoring Response: 4/4/4

As Lisa Murkowski demonstrates in "Introduction of the Bipartisan Sportsmen's Act," sporting activities such as hunting and fishing should be fostered by Congress. However, the significance of Murkowski's chosen issue does not end there; for her, the Congressionally-protected activities of sportsmen and -women are beneficial to American society at large. Murkowski effectively establishes and substantiates her argument about the necessity of legislative protections by employing key statistics, by using references to her own deep involvement, and by presenting her opponents as suspicious and potentially destructive.

Murkowski crafts a rigorously empirical argument by incorporating statistics that illuminate her main topic: the productive, cricual role of sportsmen in society. In the course of her discussion, she asserts that

"Sportsmen and women spent roughly $90 billion in 2013" and that such expenditures are an asset to "travel industry, to the hospitality industry, and to many other sectors of our economy." This information is intended to show the reader that sporting activities confer concrete economic benefits, and to do so in a manner that leaves little doubt that Murkowski is deploying concrete, verifiable data. On account of Murkowski's evidence, readers can understand that protecting sportsmen equates, quite clearly, with protecting valuable industries. Yet Murkowski's use of statistical proof does not stop here; she continues on to explain that sportsmen's purchases in Alaska "created more than $439 million in retail sales and $195 million in salaries and wages. Hunting in Alaska also brings in over $53 million to State and local governments each year." With such a quotation, Murkowski expands her thesis outward to assert that even a single state can find its economy bolstered and enhanced by sportsmen. The true significance of such information is that it statistically shows why the government—a beneficiary of sportsmen's endeavors—should protect these constituents.

Beyond articulating her ideas using statistical measures, Murkowski also employs language that is perfect for indicating her credible, involved stance. For instance, Murkowski states that "For many of us, outdoor activities are a tradition that is passed down from generation to generation.." As an author, she is attuned to the need to situate herself within the resonate way of life that she is defending. Yet Murkowski later puts a rhetoric of commitment to another use, directing attention to "a bill that I have championed for several years, the Recreational Fishing and Hunting Heritage and Opportunities Act..." With this quotation,

Murkowski moves from aligning herself with productive sportsmen and -women to the new tactic of explaning that she is dedicated, constructive advocate. Here, she appeals to a reader's natural admiration for a proactive approach based on candid, constructive government measures.

Murkowski's writing is also guided by another especially potent tactic, the phrasing that construes her opponents as illogical and unreliable. As Murkowski explains, her legislation is designed "is necessary to push back against some extreme environmental groups." This vivid statement helps Murkowski to establish her adversaries as unbalanced, while construing Murkowski's own legislation as thoughtful and necessary. Building on this important sentence, Murkowski then explains that these "extreme" groups demand rules and ependitures that might make it impossible for sportsmen "to continue participating in outdoor activities." Murkowski, on the basis of this evidence, is no headstrong demagogue. Instead, she proves through information of this sort that she is a decisive yet balanced advocate of moderate measures; she is well aware of the radical, harmful ideas of her opposition and can offer a principled stance against extremes.

With her adept uses of rhetorical devices, Murkowski affirms to her readers that legislative safeguards for outdoors pursuits are of supreme importance. Her instances of statistics, expert involvement, and counter-argumentation are expertly designed to sway her audience, enabling readers to engage the issue of sportsmen's rights in terms of both evidence and credible, conscientous testimony.

Practice Essay #3

Adapted from Former United States President Barack Obama. First State of the Union Address, delivered January 27, 2010.

1 One year ago, I took office amid two wars, an economy rocked by a severe recession, a financial system on the verge of collapse, and a government deeply in debt. Experts from across the political spectrum warned that if we did not act, we might face a second depression. So we acted, immediately and aggressively. And one year later, the worst of the storm has passed.

2 But the devastation remains: One in 10 Americans still can't find work. Many businesses have shuttered. Home values have declined. Small towns and rural communities have been hit especially hard. And for those who'd already known poverty, life has become that much harder. . .

3 So I know the anxieties that are out there right now. They're not new. These struggles are the reason I ran for president. These struggles are what I've witnessed for years in places like Elkhart, Indiana, Galesburg, Illinois.

4 I hear about them in the letters that I read each night. The toughest to read are those written by children, asking why they have to move from their home, asking when their mom or dad will be able to go back to work. . .

5 We face big and difficult challenges. And what the American people hope—what they deserve—is for all of us, Democrats and Republicans, to work through our differences, to overcome the numbing weight of our politics, for while

the people who sent us here have different backgrounds, different stories, different beliefs, the anxieties they face are the same, the aspirations they hold are shared: a job that pays the bills, a chance to get ahead, most of all, the ability to give their children a better life.

6 You know what else they share? They share a stubborn resilience in the face of adversity. After one of the most difficult years in our history, they remain busy building cars and teaching kids, starting businesses and going back to school. They're coaching Little League and helping their neighbors.

7 One woman wrote to me and said, "We are strained but hopeful, struggling but encouraged." It's because of this spirit—this great decency and great strength—that I have never been more hopeful about America's future than I am tonight. . .

8 Our most urgent—our most urgent task upon taking office was to shore up the same banks that helped cause this crisis. It was not easy to do. And if there's one thing that has unified Democrats and Republicans—and everybody in between— it's that we all hated the bank bailout. I hated it. . . It was about as popular as a root canal.

9 But when I ran for president, I promised I wouldn't just do what was popular, I would do what was necessary. And if we had allowed the meltdown of the financial system, unemployment might be double what it is today. . . Now, as we stabilized the financial system, we also took steps to get our economy growing again, save as many jobs as possible, and help Americans who'd become unemployed.

10 That's why we extended or increased unemployment benefits for more than 18 million Americans, made health insurance

155

65 percent cheaper for families who get their coverage through COBRA, and passed 25 different tax cuts. . .

10 As a result, millions of Americans had more to spend on gas and food and other necessities, all of which helped businesses keep more workers. And we haven't raised income taxes by a single dime on a single person, not a single dime. Now, because of the steps we took, there are about 2 million Americans working right now who would otherwise be unemployed. Two-hundred-thousand work in construction and clean energy. Three-hundred-thousand are teachers and other education workers. Tens of thousands are cops, firefighters, correctional officers, first responders.

11 And we're on track to add another 1.5 million jobs to this total by the end of the year . . . After two years of recession, the economy is growing again. Retirement funds have started to gain back some of their value. Businesses are beginning to invest again, and slowly, some are starting to hire again.

12 But I realize that, for every success story, there are other stories, of men and women who wake up with the anguish of not knowing where their next paycheck will come from, who send out resumes week after week and hear nothing in response. That is why jobs must be our No. 1 focus in 2010, and that's why I'm calling for a new jobs bill tonight.

Write an essay in which you explain how Barack Obama builds an argument to persuade his audience that the American government can combat economic hardship. In your essay, analyze how Obama uses one or more of the features listed in the box above (or features of your own choice) to strengthen the logic and persuasiveness of his argument. Be sure that your analysis focuses on the most relevant features of the passage.

Your essay should not explain whether you agree with Obama's claims, but rather explain how Obama builds an argument to persuade his audience.

High-Scoring Response: 4/4/4

As Barack Obama demonstrates in his "First State of the Union Address," the American government can proactively address economic turmoil. However, the significance of Obama's chosen issue does not end there; for him, the government is aware of civilian suffering and persistent in its efforts to do good. Obama effectively establishes and substantiates his argument about the government's influence in economic life by setting forth pragmatic solutions, by using personal anecdotes, and by calling forth the emotions of pride and optimism.

Obama crafts a practical argument by incorporating solutions and recommendations that illuminate his main topic: the power of the U.S. government to promote a healthy economy. In the course of his discussion, he asserts that when presented with the prospect of a "second depression" his administration "acted, immediately and aggressively. And one year later, the worst of the storm has passed." This information is intended to show the reader that the U.S. government can be proactive even against daunting odds, and to do so in a manner that underscores how well-suited Obama's solutions (bailouts, tax cuts, unemployment benefits) are to avoiding historical crises—namely, the "second depression." On account of Obama's evidence, readers can understand there is an indisputable record of the government's ability to act swiftly for the common good.. Yet Obama's use of valid solutions does not stop here; he continues on to explain that his government "extended or increased unemployment benefits for more than 18 million Americans, made health insurance 65 percent cheaper for families who get their coverage through COBRA, and passed 25 different tax cuts." With such a quotation,

Obama expands his thesis outward to assert that the solutions he promotes take a variety of well-organized forms. Yet the true significance of such information is that it shows that there is hard, statistical evidence for the government's ability to improve its citizens' lives through tax cuts and public aid.

Beyond articulating his ideas using clear solutions, Obama also employs language that is perfect for incorporating personal and anecdotal accounts. For instance, Obama states that he has witnessed economic struggles "in places like Elkhart, Indiana, Galesburg, Illinois" and hears about hardships "in the letters that I read each night." As an author, he is attuned to the human costs of economic trouble—and puts a human face on the issue to make it accessible to his readers. Yet Obama later puts anecdotes to another use, explaining that "One woman wrote to me and said, "We are strained but hopeful, struggling but encouraged." With this quotation, Obama moves from offering stories of hardship to the new tactic of narrating, in accessible anecdotal terms, how economic hardship can be overcome by both government and individual effort. Here, he appeals to the reader's sense of specificity and emotion, using the "one woman" to put a human face on vast economic issue.

Obama's writing is also guided by another especially potent tactic, the use of an optimistic, inspirational narrative tone. As Obama explains, describing his fellow Americans: "After one of the most difficult years in our history, they remain busy building cars and teaching kids, starting businesses and going back to school." This forward-thinking statement helps Obama to establish a tone of faith in American enterprise that is both candid and innately positive. Building on this important sentence, Obama then explains that "we're on track to add another 1.5 million jobs to this total by the end of the year . . . After two years of recession, the economy is growing again." Obama, on the basis of this evidence, is no hyper-critical naysayer. Instead, he proves through information of this sort that he is aware of difficulties yet undaunted by challenges; he is well aware of the power of optimism, when complemented by realism, as the ideal mindset for discussing an economic turnaround.

With his adept uses of rhetorical devices, Obama affirms to his readers that the U.S. government can proactiely fight an array of economic hardships. His instances of firm solutions, personal testimony, and well-justified optimism are expertly designed to sway his audience, enabling readers to engage the issue of American economic struggle in terms of both practical reasoning and reassuring emotion.

Practice Essay #4

Adapted from J. Morris Kirby. "Get Lost, Young Man, Get Lost" Copyright 2017 PrepVantage Publishing (November 2017).

1 The first time I saw Italy, I was ready to drop, exhausted from fifteen solid hours of flights and layovers. It was the summer between my sophomore and junior years of college; although my knowledge of the language was limited mostly to a dog-eared "Conversational Italian: Beginner Level" guidebook, I had somehow convinced the small, New England liberal arts college that I attended to give me an undergraduate research grant in art history. I would see the painterly glories of Florence, Venice, and Milan. First, though, I had to get from from Florence airport to bus terminal to youth hostel, all with an Italian vocabulary of about 25 words.

2 I made it somehow. I found a cab driver who took me the "long route" (meaning: he ran up unnecessary mileage to increase his fare). Yet the "long route" included a nighttime view of Florence's central cathedral—a masterpiece of light and dark stonework, illuminated by ghostly golden light—that I will never forget.

3 Yes, I did see the masterpieces of Florence, Venice, and Milan. Yet what has stayed with me, in the 25 years since then, is the sensation of being kind of young and kind of dumb, and really discovering the world outside my hometown and my campus for the first time.

4 It's a wonderful sensation. It's also a sensation, weirdly, that too few of today's young people crave.

5 On the basis of the most recent figures, college students just

162

don't seem to care much about adventuring abroad: a paltry 10% (maximum) of U.S. undergraduates pursue study abroad experiences. The number of students going abroad does grow year-over-year by roughly 2-3%, at least as of 2013, but is that really enough to bring the American "millennial" generation into a globalized world?

6 According to the parents, it isn't. Just last year [2017], a study released by HSBC and publicized by CNN revealed that 36% of American parents approve of the idea of their kids going abroad for college—not simply research travel like mine, but actual, enrolled semesters. How strange it is: mom and pop are more interested in a semester in France or Brazil or Japan than the student who would actually enjoy these new destinations. Are American students simply afraid to leave their comfort zones, no matter how many gourmet meals or World Cup bonanzas the rest of the world has to offer? The young soul in me sure hopes not.

7 In fact, there could be a better explanation for these disparities: American college students—who are undoubtedly ambitious—may doubt that foreign travel confers any real benefit. It seems illogical, of course, to leave your home university and all the internships, research facilities, and seasoned professors it has to offer. But staying aggressively on-campus will deprive a student of benefits—immersion in a foreign language, firsthand appreciation of cultural differences, new international student colleagues—that are harder to glean if a student stays stateside.

8 Yet students and parents in other countries do grasp the importance of international exchange to a college education. In the same HSBC survey, over 50% of parents in China and India expressed clear support for having their sons and daughters study outside their home countries. The implications here don't concern the arts and humanities

163

alone, either. No, the real situation is that fast-developing world powers in science and engineering are creating better-connected, better-adapted workforces—exposing their best students to Chinese or Indian *and* American labs, industries, and specialists.

9 If travel will solve the problem, then getting students out of the country has never been more urgent. A 2014-2015 study that originated with the Electronic Testing Service found that, among industrialized nations, the U.S. is situated right near the bottom in both mathematical and problem-solving aptitudes. Of course, the American education system is in many ways divided between moneyed high-achievers and less affluent low-achievers. But aggressively directing smart yet less-privileged students towards world-class, bargain-priced universities in Canada and Scandinavia can address *that* problem too.

10 Study abroad often looks like the domain of dreamers, idlers, and architecture snobs. It isn't: it makes sense even if the only logic that will sway you is cold, hard economics. That shouldn't be the only logic, though. So much of great mathematical, scientific, or technological thought is rooted in imagination. It's time for American students to let their imaginations wander, and wander across the world.

Write an essay in which you explain how J. Morris Kirby builds an argument to persuade his audience that American colleges should promote travel abroad among their students. In your essay, analyze how Kirby uses one or more of the features listed in the box above (or features of your own choice) to strengthen the logic and persuasiveness of his argument. Be sure that your analysis focuses on the most relevant features of the passage.

Your essay should not explain whether you agree with Kirby's claims, but rather explain how Kirby builds an argument to persuade his audience.

High-Scoring Response: 4/4/4

As J. Morris Kirby demonstrates in "Get Lost, Young Man, Get Lost," institutions of American higher education should encourage study abroad opportunities. However, the significance of Kirby's chosen issue does not end there; for him, students can gain transformative new skills and perspectives through such travel. Kirby effectively substantiates his argument about academic travel overseas by employing contrasts between wise and problematic stances, by explaining concrete benefits, and by appealing to a desire for pleasure and excitement.

Kirby crafts an assured argument by incorporating contrasts that illuminate his main topic: the advisability of international education for Americans. In the course of his discussion, he asserts that "10% (maximum) of U.S. undergraduates pursue study abroad" while "36% of American parents approve of the idea of their kids going abroad for college." This information is intended to show the reader the disparity between different generations, and to do so in a manner that clarifies the optimal position. On account of Kirby's evidence, readers can understand that young people have unwisely placed themselves at odd with parental figures who support study abroad by a larger share. Yet Kirby's use of pointed contrast does not stop here; he continues on to explain that "fast-developing world powers in science and engineering [China and India] are creating better-connected, better-adapted workforces," than America is. With such a quotation, Kirby expands his thesis outward to assert that American young people who eschew study abroad are shortsighted in a second respect. The true significance of such information is that it articulates the contrast between dyamically international students from China and India, and American students who act against logical self-interest.

Beyond articulating his ideas using juxtaposed perspectives, Kirby also employs benefit-based reasoning that is perfect for emphasizing the urgency of journey-based education. For instance, Kirby states that travel abroad confers "immersion in a foreign language, firsthand appreciation of cultural differences, [and] new international student colleagues." As an author, he is attuned to the large array of indisputable benefits that await students who venture beyond the U.S. Yet Kirby later puts the consideration of benefits to another use, calling on America to direct "less-privileged students towards world-class, bargain-priced universities in Canada and Scandinavia." With this quotation, Kirby moves from highlighting culture and collaboration to the new tactic of citing economic conundrums that enrollment in foreign colleges can address head-on. Here, he appeals to some of his most logical and demanding readers—those who seek financial and empirical justification for an agenda based on travel.

Kirby's writing is also guided by another especially potent tactic, the use of exicited, pleasing emotional appeals. As Kirby explains, he as a young man was thrilled by European travel that involved "really discovering the world outside my hometown and my campus for the first time." This ebullient statement helps Kirby to establish a tone of candid passion for travel, helping the reader to feel the visceral allure of journeys abroad. Building on this important sentence, Kirby then explains that study abroad, even today, raises the possibility of the "gourmet meals or World Cup bonanzas the rest of the world has to offer." Kirby, on the basis of this evidence, is no austere and unapproachable critic. Instead, he proves through information of this sort that he is eager to transmit the joy of studying outside the U.S. to younger readers; he is well aware of the power of pleasurable details in leading his audience to embrace the right set of values.

With his adept uses of rhetorical devices, Kirby affirms to his readers that study abroad options are essential for undergraduates in the United States. His instances of contrasts, beneficial outcomes, and pleasing, adventurous description are expertly designed to sway his audience, enabling readers to engage the issue of student travel in terms of both reasoning and emotion.

Appendix D:

Essay Checklists
Additional Copies

This final appendix is designed to give you additional copies of the Writing Checklist that appeared in Chapter 10. As you complete more essays, you should return to this checklist to make sure that your writing style is improving over time.

You can also download a printable version of the checklist at PrepVantageBooks.com. Just click on the "SAT Essay" link at the top and go to "Practice Documents."

Checklists begin on the next page

Date: _____   # 1

Essay: _____

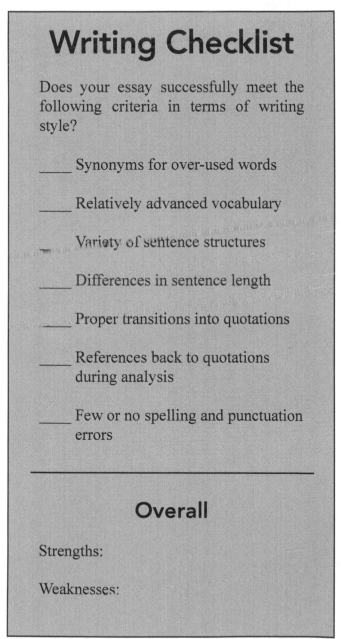

Writing Checklist

Does your essay successfully meet the following criteria in terms of writing style?

_____ Synonyms for over-used words

_____ Relatively advanced vocabulary

_____ Variety of sentence structures

_____ Differences in sentence length

_____ Proper transitions into quotations

_____ References back to quotations during analysis

_____ Few or no spelling and punctuation errors

Overall

Strengths:

Weaknesses:

Date: _____

Essay: _____

Writing Checklist

Does your essay successfully meet the following criteria in terms of writing style?

_____ Synonyms for over-used words

_____ Relatively advanced vocabulary

_____ Variety of sentence structures

_____ Differences in sentence length

_____ Proper transitions into quotations

_____ References back to quotations during analysis

_____ Few or no spelling and punctuation errors

Overall

Strengths:

Weaknesses:

Date: _____   **#3**

Essay: _____

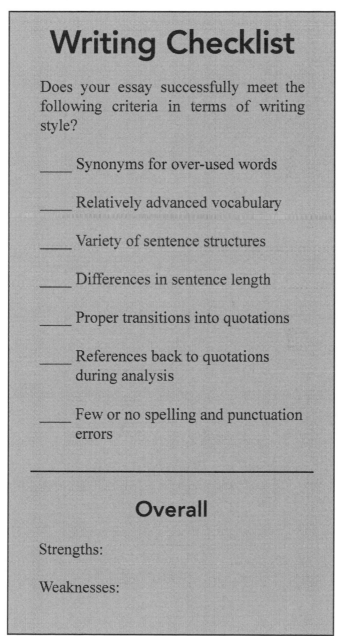

Writing Checklist

Does your essay successfully meet the following criteria in terms of writing style?

_____ Synonyms for over-used words

_____ Relatively advanced vocabulary

_____ Variety of sentence structures

_____ Differences in sentence length

_____ Proper transitions into quotations

_____ References back to quotations during analysis

_____ Few or no spelling and punctuation errors

Overall

Strengths:

Weaknesses:

Date: _____   **#4**

Essay: _____

Writing Checklist

Does your essay successfully meet the following criteria in terms of writing style?

_____ Synonyms for over-used words

_____ Relatively advanced vocabulary

_____ Variety of sentence structures

_____ Differences in sentence length

_____ Proper transitions into quotations

_____ References back to quotations during analysis

_____ Few or no spelling and punctuation errors

Overall

Strengths:

Weaknesses:

Date: _____   **#5**

Essay: _____

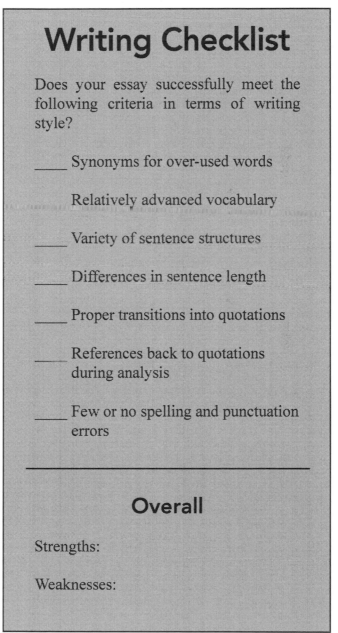

Writing Checklist

Does your essay successfully meet the following criteria in terms of writing style?

_____ Synonyms for over-used words

_____ Relatively advanced vocabulary

_____ Variety of sentence structures

_____ Differences in sentence length

_____ Proper transitions into quotations

_____ References back to quotations during analysis

_____ Few or no spelling and punctuation errors

Overall

Strengths:

Weaknesses:

Made in the USA
Middletown, DE
09 August 2019